D1568355

What people are saying about

Business Relationship Management for the Digital Enterprise

"*Vaughan Merlyn's book has quickly become my 'go-to' reference as I work with IT organizations looking to become more strategic within their companies. Vaughan wonderfully captures his extensive and powerful learnings from his successful career into an easy-to-read and understand guide that will benefit anyone looking to lead IT into the future. How fortunate we are to get access to these kernels of wisdom from one who has blazed the trails in the exciting area of Business Relationship Management. And as a bonus, you'll learn how to 'rock' like Vaughan… again providing additional fun and insight to business. Get this book and be inspired.*"
Kip Fanta, CBRM, Principal, Kip Fanta Group

"*Recognizing and encouraging the convergence of Business and Information Technology introduces new opportunities for organizations in digital innovation. This book is a must-read for individuals facing these challenges, including IT and business executives that lead the transition, but more importantly the Business Relationship Manager, who is uniquely qualified and positioned to provide the Renaissance-esque competencies for this convergence. Welcome to the Renaissance!*"
Ric Golemon, Managing Director, Bluetone Consulting Associates, Inc.

"*Vaughan's use of vignettes from his personal experiences add color and flavor to his holistic approach to moving towards a digital enterprise. He surfaces relationships between such critical areas as Lean, Agile, Business Relationship Management, and Organizational Change Management for successfully delivering digital transformation. His attainable, common sense approach makes this required reading for all levels of IT Management.*"
Arnie Wetherill, CBRM

"A must read in your BRM Library. Vaughan's book acknowledges the challenges and road-blocks that a BRM professional will face. The unique voice of this book is that it identifies root causes from culture to processes to human tendencies. It moves away from a one-size solution fits all to helping you understand environment and suggesting a number of possible solutions. The ultimate goal—realizing the promises of digitization by being an effective BRM in today's digital enterprise."
Leanne McGiveron, BRMP Director, Business Relationship Management

"Vaughan's success as a highly-regarded management consultant comes in no small part from his keen eye, quick wit, and his ability to connect dots—talents every BRM or other leader must develop to be effective. They are all on display in this book. If you are involved in or interested in digitization, it is an essential addition to your library. Vaughan captures his magical charisma in his book, so you will not only learn from it, you will enjoy it. I know I did!"
Roy Youngman, Chief Knowledge Manager, BRM Institute

"Vaughan is a luminary in the Business Relationship Management world. He's our Beatles, Rolling Stones, James Brown, and Elvis Presley all rolled up into one! This book is a must read for BRMs and IT Leaders alike. There is great wisdom and guidance on a host of topics that practitioners and leaders will find tremendously helpful. In addition, hidden within all the great Digital and BRM knowledge in this book, is a Master Class on Collaborative Change. If your organization is thinking about making a large-scale change or is in the midst of one, you must read this chapter! It will revolutionize your approach to organizational change."
Aaron Monroe, Board Director, BRM Institute

"Chock full of wisdom, as well as critical concepts, practical techniques, and illuminating examples. This book should be ever-present on the desk of every BRM and CIO! Vaughan takes this most complex challenge of business relationship management and breaks it down into the elements that are key to your success. My advice: Open brain, insert the content of this book, and be on your way to achieving BRM success!"
Sheila Smith, President, Omega Point Consulting

"Many talk about digital transformation, but few have the experience, perspective, and insights to provide such a valuable resource to IT professionals at all levels who seek to make this huge change. As the recognized Godfather of Business Relationship Management, no one is better suited to act as a guide to the new world of IT."
Ronn Faigen, Board Director, BRM Institute

"Full of insights. Vaughan Merlyn delivers his wisdom culled from a fifty-year career. A must read for aspiring Business Relationship Managers and those already practicing the craft."
Steve Plante, Vice-President, Customer Experience, PeopleProductive

Business Relationship Management for the Digital Enterprise

Strategies for managing IT to meet
the digital challenges facing enterprises
now and in the future

Vaughan Merlyn

Published by The Merlyn Group
Atlanta, Georgia, USA

ISBN: 978-984737383
1. non-fiction , 2. business & economics, 3. computers, 4. author, 5.title

Library of Congress Cataloging-in-Publication data is available upon request.

First Edition, January, 2019
10 9 8 7 6 5 4 3 2 1

*To the world's Business Relationship Managers
for their impact on the business value realized from
investments in information and information technology*

Contents

Illustrations & Charts

Foreword

By Aaron Barnes, CEO and Co-founder of Business Relationship Management Institute

This is a book about the evolution of Information Technology (IT)—evolution in the ways that people, information, and technology are both led and leveraged, and evolution in the nature of organizational change itself. These topics are brought to life through the lens of a fifty-year career in IT, thirty years of that in research and management consulting. Twelve years of blogging have focused and strengthened that perspective, and shone a spotlight on IT leadership, IT operating models and the emergence of Business Relationship Management as a catalyst for a new approach to managing IT.

Evolution associated with IT has been with us since the earliest days of computerization. But most of the direct impacts of that change have been felt by the IT professional, who has had to learn new programming languages, new methods and tools and new ways of engaging the so-called *end user* of IT. Today, when we talk about the digital enterprise, we are referring to changes that have far reaching impact—well beyond the IT professional. In some ways, the end user is becoming a proxy for the IT professional.

This is a very different form of IT transformation from those that we have experienced in the past. It is not simply evolution of the IT organization. It is evolution that permeates every corner of business and industry and that reaches far into marketplaces and ecosystems. To coin a phrase, "This is not your grandfather's IT transformation!"

In April 2019, McKinsey's Global Survey on digital and analytics transformations across the business landscape found that about eight in ten respondents said their organizations had begun digital transformations but that just fourteen percent had made and sustained performance improvements. Just three percent reported success at sustaining their change. Clearly, while digitization can offer substantial benefits, digital transformations present unique challenges that place these benefits out of reach for many enterprises. Vaughan takes time to address some of these challenges and how they can be mitigated.

While others have documented aspects of the IT management journey, or have postulated about emerging management models, none have approached the subject with the breadth of context, depth of analysis and the focus on the digital enterprise you will find here. Richly illustrated with anecdotes from the author's illustrious career in IT, the book is both illuminating and entertaining.

To give you a bit of our history, I first became aware of Vaughan through his blog, IT Organization Circa 2017, and subsequently through his engagement in and contributions to the Professional Business Relationship Managers LinkedIn group I started in 2011. Vaughan accepted my invitation to co-moderate the group later that year. I subsequently engaged him to spend a day with my BRM team, providing a briefing and an open discussion about the BRM role and capability.

As the Professional Business Relationship Managers Linkedin group continued to grow, there was an organic request from the group to make BRM real, to create standards and certifications, and bring to life a single global BRM community where the members could network and help each other grow. From all that, Business Relationship Management Institute, Inc was founded as a non-profit organization dedicated to inspiring, promoting, and developing excellence in Business Relationship Management across the globe.

This book sets the stage by describing the shifts in the IT landscape over the last fifty years and how changes in computing platforms led to the evolution of IT management models. It introduces and explains the genesis of the Business-IT Maturity Model—a tool that is central to an understanding of how business demand for IT increases in quantity and quality as IT supply matures.

Here you will find a framework for understanding the forces behind digitization, and the tenets of IT operating models and what these must accomplish in the age of the digital business. It introduces the role and capabilities of Business Relationship Management and describes how these can accelerate the convergence of business and IT to forever eliminate the notorious Business-IT alignment gap.

Vaughan differentiates IT management from IT leadership and discusses the nature of

IT leadership that is necessary for the digital enterprise. He poses provocative scenarios about alternate IT realities, and raises profound questions about reactive and proactive approaches to IT leadership for the digital enterprise.

He explains the differences between Business-IT alignment and Business-IT convergence, why alignment was never an appropriate goal, and why convergence is becoming the reality behind successful digital enterprises.

Vaughan introduces us to Business Relationship Management as a role, as a discipline, and as a capability. He describes how BRM is an organizational innovation that can accelerate the shift from IT as a means to solve problems, to IT as a driver of opportunity creation and value realization.

He develops this theme to illuminate the ways that Business Relationship Management can be the key to creating a Business-IT converged operating model—one that is optimized for driving business value. He examines the implications of the converged operating model for today's IT organization, and offers new ways to think about diverse IT capabilities as dispersed and distributed throughout the digital enterprise and, in so doing, bringing shadow IT out of the shadows and into the light.

Vaughan shares his research into BRM time allocation, and how BRMs can rebalance their activities to be a more effective catalysts for Business-IT convergence and the transition to the digital enterprise.

In his discussion about transforming the IT operating model, Vaughan drills into the nature of operating models, and the components and characteristics of a high performing operating model. A key to the emerging digital IT operating model is organizational clarity, a concept Vaughan explores in some depth, and one that he connects back to IT capability maturity. He not only examines the ways an IT operating model must change for the digital enterprise, he also examines how digital capabilities allow new ways to design and transition to digital operating models.

Vaughan takes on the challenging topic of organizational and cultural evolution, and shows us how much of the conventional change management wisdom is deeply flawed in today's organizational context. He examines a new collaborative model for change—one that is far more natural, less disruptive, and designed with the digital business in mind—both as a target of organizational change and as a means of achieving it.

Playing to one of his greatest strengths as a storyteller, and drawing on his vast array of life experiences, Vaughan entertains and enlightens the reader with "Leadership Lessons from the Performing Arts". He draws from his experiences in amateur dramatics and as a rock and roll musician. This chapter reinforces the importance of taking time away from the job to explore hobbies, while being mindful about the many connections between leisure activities and work.

In his music, Vaughan finds lessons about team building, organizational change, active listening, multi-tasking, learning, and risk taking. He even drills into motor cycling and scuba diving as sources of wisdom that can be applied to many aspects of work and life.

Preface: A Readers Guide

I launched my blog—IT Organization Circa 2017—in September 2007, and wrote 451 blog posts over a 12-year period. These posts were inspired by client consulting engagements, reader's questions and comments, participation in several LinkedIn groups, and multi-company research programs regarding IT management. The book is built upon an edited selection of those posts.

As a management consultant, I had tracked and participated in the major technology shifts that impacted IT management. Over time, I became increasing focused on IT operating models and the emerging Business Relationship Management (BRM) role and capability.

In 2013, I cofounded Business Relationship Management Institute as a non-profit member-based organization and further deepened my involvement in the rapidly growing BRM global community.

I came to realize through my contacts with numerous BRMs, participation in the annual BRMConnect conferences, and involvement with the BRM Institute member's Online Campus and Interactive Body of Knowledge, that organizations were struggling with certain aspects of defining and delivering on the BRM promise. I knew that many of the issues people were facing were addressed somewhere among those 451 blog posts.

At the same time, I recognized that pointing everyone to my blog and expecting them to find the relevant pages was not a strong value proposition, so the idea of this book was born. Its content was drawn from broad experience in the field as well as twelve years of blogging about BRM and the IT management context in which it exists.

Getting The Most From This Book

The reader can certainly read this book sequentially from start to finish. But given the fact that it is largely drawn from twelve years of blogging, there are other options for approaching this book:

- Review the Table of Contents on pages 1-6 and select topics to enjoy in a sequence that fits your needs.
- Flip through the book to find topics and vignettes in the blue story-teller boxes that catch your eye.
- Peruse the Index stating on page 219, and use the book as a reference source as you move through your enterprise digitization and BRM journey.

Who Should Read This Book

Based upon my interactions with the BRM and IT leadership communities, I had several distinct audiences in mind when writing *Business Relationship Management* for the Digital Enterprise.

Those Already in the BRM Role

This book should help those already in the BRM role, or considering a transition into that role, or working closely with the role, including Business Analysts, Project and Program Managers, and Enterprise Architects:

- Become an effective and valued catalyst for digitization through a better understanding of how the BRM role serves the goal and outcomes of digitization, how to effectively organize and staff BRM capabilities, and how to avoid the common traps that derail BRM success
- Appreciate the crucial skills and qualities demanded of a successful BRM who possesses the credibility, gravitas, and techniques that empower them with access, influence, and relationships necessary to be a key player in the digitization movement
- Improve productivity and the resource utilization of IT colleagues by understanding the value of shifting the organization's focus from projects, services, and activities to business value realization, Business-IT convergence, and digital innovation
- Strengthen personal status and job security by creating measurable organizational improvement, and catalyzing game-changing business strategy supported by a digital, Business-IT converged operating model
- Chart a career growth path that anticipates and participates in the emerging digitization movement

Executives and IT Leaders Considering the Introduction of BRM

In addition to the points raised above, this book should help executives and IT leaders considering the introduction of BRM capability:

- Strengthen Business-IT relationships by learning how to introduce and develop a BRM capability that visibly increases business value realized from information and IT
- Learn how to improve the customer experience of everyone who depends upon information and IT by leveraging BRM to re-shape the IT operating model into one that drives Business-IT convergence and facilitates the digital enterprise
- Catalyze a potentially game-changing Business-IT strategy, and deliver against that strategy by understanding the business and IT implications of digitization, and how to lead colleagues and business partners into and through a digital transition

BRM Advocates in Federal, State, and Local Government

In addition to the points presented above, this book should help BRM advocates in federal, state, and local government better understand the characteristics of the BRM role and capability, the necessary conditions for success, and ways to introduce BRM into their organizations.

Management Consultants and Others Interested in Helping Organizations with BRM

In addition to the points presented above, this book should help management consultants and others interested in helping organizations with BRM deployment and performance improvement appreciate the challenges and issues faced by BRMs and their advocates, and gain broader insight into ways that these challenges are being overcome across industries and governmental organizations around the world.

Educators Interested in Introducing Latest Trends in Technology

In addition to the points presented above, this book should help educators interested in introducing the latest trends in technology in their classrooms to better prepare their students to thrive in today's digital enterprise.

Introduction: Business Relationship Management and the Digital Enterprise

The emerging digital enterprise will depend on an effective Business Relationship Manager role and capability in order to demolish today's barriers.

Overview

This book is for those interested in the management of Information and Information Technology (IT) for the digital enterprise. It examines how Business Relationship Management (BRM), an organizational innovation that first appeared in the 1990s and has been gaining traction globally, can accelerate the time-to-value from digitization.

Based on lessons from a 50-year career in IT, the book draws from an intensive 30+ years as a management consultant and 12 years of blogging. The blog posts were inspired by client consulting engagements, reader's questions and comments, participation in several LinkedIn groups, and many multi-company research programs.

In compiling posts for the book, I selected, edited and integrated the most relevant posts and organized them into a Foreword, Introduction, eight chapters and an Afterword. I believe the topics discussed here are relevant to any organization large enough to have or be considering a dedicated IT group. It would be a valuable addition to a Freshman level college course.

Business Relationship Management and the Digital Enterprise

The book is based on lessons from a fifty year career in IT spanning from computer hardware design, software development, marketing, sales, corporate management, research, and management consulting. More specifically, the book draws from twelve years of blogging.

My blog, launched in September 2007, was titled IT Organization Circa 2017 and focused on the major shifts in the world of IT management, looking ten years ahead. Here's part of my very first post from September 21, 2007:

> I named this blog IT Organization Circa 2017 in an attempt to position the domain of interest: what will the IT Organization inside businesses, governments and other organized entities look like in 10 years (2017) and how did they get there? I picked 2017 as a time-frame that allows much change to be possible and that I will (statistically, and hopefully) be around to see.
>
> I've worked with IT organizations for about 35 years, in the US and internationally. I've been involved with dozens of multi-client research programs that examined IT effectiveness, business value realization and organizational change. Over that time, I've watched (and hopefully, helped) as the IT profession evolved from mainframe to the Internet and from Machine Code to JavaScript.
>
> I've watched as the most valued IT skills evolved accordingly from programming, to business analysis, to business relationship management and innovation. I've watched as the IT organization came out of the shadows as a perceived necessary cost to a strategic enabler. Where does it go next? How does it get there? How does the line get drawn and redrawn over time between what the IT organization does for the busi-

3

ness with IT, and what the business does for themselves with IT?

I hope that this blog will become something of a focal point for engaging in a global conversation about how IT organizations evolve over the next 10 years.

The blog was very much a stream of consciousness—discrete posts inspired by client consulting engagements, reader's questions and comments, and many multi-company research programs I was part of. The posts were generally grounded in observations about the evolution of the IT organization, sometimes branching off into my hobbies with lessons from the performing arts.

In compiling the posts for this book, I have selected and edited the most relevant posts and organized them into an Introduction, eight chapters and an Afterword. I believe the topics discussed in this book are relevant to any entity large enough to have a dedicated IT organization.

Chapter 1: The Shifting IT Landscape. A summary of the major shifts in IT management over the last 50 years and an over-arching framework for understanding the evolution of IT that provides a context for the book

Chapter 2: Why Business-IT Maturity Is So Important. An introduction to a Business-IT Maturity Model, an examination of how business demand maturity and IT supply maturity have evolved over time, and the implications for future IT management approaches

Chapter 3: IT Leadership For The Digital Enterprise. Issues pertinent to business and IT leaders, regardless of job title or position

Chapter 4: Managing IT In A Digital Enterprise. A review of digital enterprise IT capability, what this means for the traditional IT organization and how new theories of organizational change are shaping future IT capabilities

Chapter 5: Business Relationship Management: Catalyst For A Digital Revolution. Issues and practices regarding the Business Relationship Management role, discipline and capability

Chapter 6: Driving Business-IT Convergence Through Business Relationships. An examination of what the future may hold for Business Relationship Management (BRM) in fostering Business-IT Convergence and stimulating business innovation

Chapter 7: Transitioning To A Digital IT Operating Model. An examination of what is meant by IT Operating Model and how this notion is being impacted by digitization. It suggests principles for Operating Model transformation

Chapter 8: Collaborative Change. Observations and ideas about organizational change based upon contemporary thinking, and tools for collaboration

Afterword: Lessons From The Performing Arts. Experiences and learnings for today's IT professional from the performing arts

Biography. Highlights of my career and how growing up in post-war London and my three distinct career phases (engineer, business leader, management consultant) have shaped my world view

Notes On Language Used In This Book

IT
The term *Information and Information Technology* reinforces that IT management is much more than managing technology. As used in this book, the abbreviation IT refers collectively to Information and IT.

IT ORGANIZATION
The tern *IT organization*, as used in this book, refers to the group that primarily manages IT capability for a larger organization or entity such as a corporation, government agency, jurisdiction, business process, and so on.

ENTERPRISE
The term *enterprise* is used for describing the broader organizational context (company, organization, division, agency, etc.)

BUSINESS AND IT
The term *business* refers to the demand side organizations whose work requires the use of information technology and IT refers to the supply side of the business, including teams responsible for delivering business and IT capabilities. Historically, the distinction between business and IT was clearly marked and the objections against merging these terms perfectly valid. This differentiation is not intended to reinforce the invisible walls between demand and supply organizations, but in the interests of clarity, it merely recognizes that business and IT have not yet converged in most organizations.

BUSINESS-IT CONVERGENCE
Business-IT convergence is the trend for IT demand and supply to become integrated. The goal of Business-IT convergence (a subject covered at length in this book) is a

worthy one, and it is the recognized intent of those who talk and act as though IT *is the business*. However, for most enterprises, the *realpolitik* is that IT and the business are *not* converged, and sometimes seem to be on different planets!

WEB 2.0 AND WEB 3.0

Web 2.0 is a loosely defined term that has gained popularity since it was invented in 1999 by Darcy DiNucci and popularized through the Web 2.0 Conference in 2004. By implication Web 1.0 (though that term didn't exist until the term Web 2.0 was invented) was essentially non-participative. Web sites were like catalogs you could browse and buy from. Web 2.0 is essentially participatory and literally turns the web into a giant computer and global information base.

With innovations such as the *Internet of Things* (IOT), machine learning, 5G networks, and more, people are starting to use the term Web 3.0 and The *Semantic Web* to describe the emerging connective intelligence platform for the future.

DIGITAL ENTERPRISE

This is a term that is currently gaining popularity as a way to describe an Enterprise (see definition above) that uses Web 2.0 and 3.0 technologies to create a competitive advantage in its internal and external operations. At the time of publication this idea is sometimes referred to as Next Generation Enterprise, Enterprise 2.0, and similar terms.

DIGITIZATION

The term *digitization* is used as a shorthand for the move towards the digital enterprise.

DIGITAL ENTERPRISE IT CAPABILITY

Digital enterprise IT capability refers to the collection of IT capabilities needed for moving towards the digital enterprise.

The Shifting IT Landscape

We must ensure that the shift to cloud computing does not repeat the mistakes that were common with the early move to distributed computing

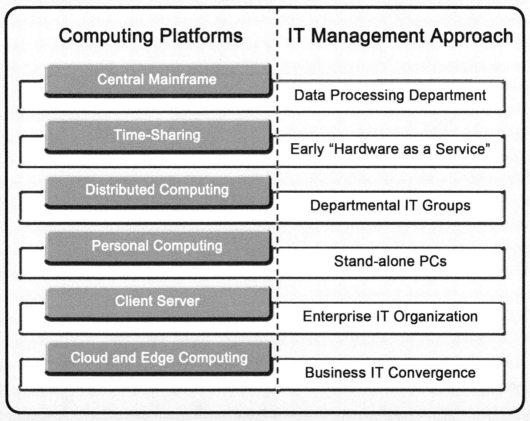

Computing Platforms	IT Management Approach
Central Mainframe	Data Processing Department
Time-Sharing	Early "Hardware as a Service"
Distributed Computing	Departmental IT Groups
Personal Computing	Stand-alone PCs
Client Server	Enterprise IT Organization
Cloud and Edge Computing	Business IT Convergence

Computing Platform and Corresponding Approaches to IT Management

The revolution in computing platforms inevitably leads to changes in approaches to IT Management

Overview

This Chapter frames the context for the book and reviews the evolution of Computing Platforms over the last 50 years and how approaches to managing IT have responded to these changes. The Chapter illustrates each Computing Platform with personal stories from my career.

The Shifting IT Landscape

The Evolution of IT and IT Management

Starting in the 1960s, the evolution in electronic building blocks led to a hardware evolution, from central mainframes to distributed computing, client-server, and to web-based architectures.

Software evolved to keep pace, shifting from custom coding to application packages, fourth generation languages, application generators and to web-based services. There's been a consistent shift in focus from hardware to software and ultimately to services.

IT management has evolved in response to these hardware and software changes. The graphic at the beginning of this Chapter (p. 9), highlights these changes.

Central Mainframe Computing

In 1970, computers were only available as large mainframe devices that would fill a huge room and require water cooling, air-conditioning, and raised floors. Mainframe computers were very expensive and needed a team of highly specialized engineers to run.

Mainframe computing was typically supported by data processing departments comprising computer operators, systems engineers, systems analysts, and programmers, managed by a data processing manager. These departments were very much isolated from the businesses that the computers served, often located in office building basements, close to the hardware but worlds away from the business. In some cases, there were literally walls separating data processing specialists from the business users that depended on them.

The Evolution of IT and IT Management: A Personal View

Over my career in IT from 1970 to 2019, seismic changes have taken place in technology and IT management. The electronic brains of computing evolved from electro-mechanical relays (yes, I actually worked on these in my first job!) to vacuum tubes (valves), to transistors, to integrated circuits, and to large scale integration.

While going through a four year Sandwich Course in the UK comprising alternate six month stints at university and industry, I experienced the misalignment between how industry was moving to new technologies more quickly than academic education was able to cover them. I was being taught about vacuum tubes and transistors at the same time I was working with integrated circuits.

The launch of the IBM PC in the 1980s turned the computing world upside down, I remember in the early 1980s asking a client's chief information officer (CIO) how he was responding to the influx of personal computers.

He looked at me like I was crazy and said, "Personal Computers are for home use. They have no place in the corporate environment. We don't allow them to be used here."

I invited him to walk with me down a couple of corridors near his headquarters office. I let him see for himself what I had seen earlier in the day: personal computers on many desks throughout the corporate campus!

Time-Sharing

In the early 1970s, a new business model for computing called time-sharing was gaining popularity. It was designed to both capitalize on the high costs of mainframes and give more people access to this powerful new business capability. Unfortunately, while making computing accessible to the masses, time-sharing demanded some technical programming skills.

Distributed Computing

Minicomputers, initially used mostly as standalone devices for applications such as process control, were first introduced in the 1960s. By the mid 1970s, minicomputers had become popular departmental computing platforms. These were soon attached to corporate mainframe computers to create distributed computing environments. The rise of distributed computing led to the first major shifts in IT management as company departments added small staffs of computer professionals to create and manage departmental applications.

The ability for departmental heads to gain control over their own computing led quickly to a proliferation of departmental computers, and the beginnings of the fragmentation of corporate computing resources. The results of this shift included islands of automation, redundant resources, duplicate business systems, and difficulties in aggregating and analyzing company data across multiple, dissimilar computing platforms, programming languages, and file structures.

Personal Computing

While small home computers, such as those from Atari, Sinclair, Commodore, were gaining popularity in the late 1970s, it was the launch of the IBM PC in 1981 that legitimized personal computers and turned the computing world upside down. Initially viewed as home computers, PCs rapidly entered the corporate environment. Personal computers appeared on many desks in organizations around the world. The PC had arrived.

Client-Server Computing

It was only a matter of time before corporate executives were demanding access to corporate data and better ways to integrate their PCs into their workflow. Soon PC-mainframe connections were added, and PC integration became commonplace as part of the move to a new computing architecture referred to as client-server computing.

More and more non-computing professionals became unofficial and often invisible players in an increasingly distributed computing workforce

With this shift, more and more non-computing professionals became unofficial and often invisible players in an increasingly distributed computing workforce. With desktop publishing software, people were able to create in hours good looking printed documents that would have demanded graphic design and technical skills and taken days or weeks.

With the introduction of the Local Area Networking in the early 1980's, and the Internet and World Wide Web in the late 1980's, the rapid transformation of computing was about to accelerate.

Cloud Computing

General business dissatisfaction with corporate IT departments followed and a sense soon developed that IT takes too long, costs too much, and delivers too little. The economic advantages of huge server farms (a collection of computer servers in a data center) led to the creation of networks of remote computer servers over the internet. This was cloud computing. It sparked the notion of *everything as a service*:

- **Software as a Service (SaaS).** Capability to use applications running on a cloud infrastructure. The consumer typically does not manage the underlying infrastructure or individual application capabilities.
- **Platform as a Service (PaaS).** Capability to deploy consumer-created or acquired applications. The consumer does not manage the underlying infrastructure but has control over the deployed applications and possibly over the application hosting environment configurations.
- **Infrastructure as a Service (IaaS).** Capability to provision processing, storage, networks, and other fundamental computing resources on a network where the consumer is able to deploy and run arbitrary software including operating systems and applications. The consumer does not manage the underlying infrastructure but has control over operating systems, storage, deployed applications, and possibly limited control of select networking components.

With cloud computing, people could gain access to computing services without making major financial, labor, or physical asset investments. They could buy by the drink and try things out before they committed significant resources.

The proverbial cat was out of the bag and, no matter what policies the CIO tried to enforce, it was not going back in again.

Why Business-IT Maturity Is So Important

2

Increasing Business-IT maturity is essential for a digital enterprise to thrive

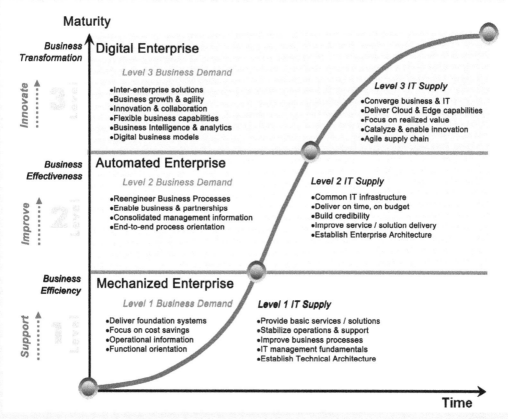

Maturity

Business Transformation

Innovate

Digital Enterprise

Level 3 Business Demand
- Inter-enterprise solutions
- Business growth & agility
- Innovation & collaboration
- Flexible business capabilities
- Business Intelligence & analytics
- Digital business models

Level 3 IT Supply
- Converge business & IT
- Deliver Cloud & Edge capabilities
- Focus on realized value
- Catalyze & enable innovation
- Agile supply chain

Business Effectiveness

Improve

Automated Enterprise

Level 2 Business Demand
- Reengineer Business Processes
- Enable business & partnerships
- Consolidated management information
- End-to-end process orientation

Level 2 IT Supply
- Common IT infrastructure
- Deliver on time, on budget
- Build credibility
- Improve service / solution delivery
- Establish Enterprise Architecture

Business Efficiency

Support

Mechanized Enterprise

Level 1 Business Demand
- Deliver foundation systems
- Focus on cost savings
- Operational information
- Functional orientation

Level 1 IT Supply
- Provide basic services / solutions
- Stabilize operations & support
- Improve business processes
- IT management fundamentals
- Establish Technical Architecture

Time

Business-IT Maturity Model

Increasing Business-IT maturity is essential for business to evolve

Overview

This Chapter introduces a Business-IT Maturity Model and examines how business demand maturity and IT supply maturity have evolved over time, how they interact and influence each other, and the implications for IT management and for business users of IT in the digital enterprise.

Why Business-IT Maturity Is So Important

Business Context

Virtually all organizations today are dependent upon IT. A rich and robust infrastructure, user friendly tools, on-demand services, processing capacity and storage space are merely table stakes for tapping the next generation of collaborative, social networking, and business capabilities.

The massive burden and resource drain from legacy systems and technologies, which often consume 80% or more of the IT budget, must be reined in to free up funds and resources for new sources of business value that are available to digital enterprises.

To do that, IT organizations must partner with business units and functions in new ways. Business and IT must have the skills to collaborate and converge, finding opportunities for product, service, process, and even business model innovation.

The Business-IT Maturity Model

The Business-IT Maturity Model (shown on p. 9) separates business demand (the appetite of business for IT and their ability to harness potential business value) and IT supply (the ability of the enterprise to satisfy that demand) and explores how these mature over time, and how they are mutually dependent. It is important to note that these do not typically move in lockstep. Sometimes demand is more mature. Other times supply leads in IT maturity.

Business demand at any point in time is a complex function of industry characteristics, market forces, business vision and leadership and many other variables. Business demand is also a function of IT supply.

Background: Business-IT Maturity Model

An important phase in my career began in 1990 with the acquisition of my small consulting and research company by Ernst & Young (E&Y) and with me becoming a Partner at the new Center for Business Innovation, located in Boston Massachusetts in a beautiful townhouse on Beacon Hill.

My portfolio at the Center was IT Effectiveness, later supplemented with Organizational Change Management. My first project was to design and lead a multi-company research initiative into IT effectiveness. We enrolled a number of leading global companies to join us, initially on a one-year exploration of IT management practices. The multi-company research program was a success and evolved into a three-year research program in IT leadership and transformation.

The Business-IT Maturity Model surfaced quickly and came to be an important calibration tool. There was nothing particularly innovative about a maturity model. Richard Nolan's five stage model was first presented in 1973 and the Software Engineering Institute contributed much to contemporary best practice with a Capability Maturity approach.

Our advancement on maturity modeling was to examine two sides of the coin—supply and demand—and how these mature and interact with each other. We also simplified the maturity concept with a three level model having found that three levels were readily understood by business executives, and served the key purposes of the model without over-complicating it or creating false precision. I am aware of several corporate boards that use Business-IT Maturity in their executive scoreboards.

The Ernst & Young Center for Business Innovation, Boston, Mass

Low supply maturity will constrain business demand (or lead to ways to work around the IT organization, such as setting up shadow IT groups and/or cloud computing).

> *If business demand gets too far ahead of IT supply, there will be a change of IT leadership*

Typically, if business demand gets too far ahead of IT supply, there will be a change of IT leadership. On the other hand, if IT supply gets too far ahead of business demand, IT will be seen to be overspending, also resulting in a change of IT leadership.

The most common patterns are at:
- Level 1. Business demand leads IT supply.
- Level 2. IT supply tends to catch up with and overtake demand.
- Level 3. Demand and supply are closely aligned.

Level 1 is mostly concerned with business efficiency, such as that achieved when clerical labor is replaced by simple automation (e.g., source data entry, transaction processing.) The primary justification for such systems is based on cost savings and satisfying demand for operational information (e.g., how many widgets were produced today?) One common characteristic of Level 1 demand is that it originates in business silos (functions and departments), and its scope is limited to these silos. This can be called the *mechanized enterprise*.

Sooner or later, the business appetite for IT goes beyond simple, silo-oriented solutions, and begins to look across silos to find and transform end-to-end business processes. Common examples include order-to-cash, procure-to-pay, and hire-to-retire.

Shifting focus from Level 1 departmental silos to Level 2 end-to-end business process creates opportunities to reengineer important business capabilities that increase business effectiveness and provide richer types of management information (e.g., which are the most profitable widgets today?) This type of process reengineering can deliver significant business value and improved customer experiences.

For the most progressive organizations, Level 2 gives way to Level 3—the domain of business transformation and the digital enterprise. This is often characterized by business models that can only exist with advanced IT capabilities, and that often become fierce competitors to traditional Level 1 and 2 establishments.

Consider, for example, how rideshare companies such as Uber and Lyft have already taken significant market share from conventional limousine, shuttle, and taxi services.

Aside from enabling new, digital business models, Level 3 is very much about innovation of products, processes and services. While Level 1 organizations know how many widgets they make in a day, and Level 2 entities also know which widgets are most profitable, Level 3 digital enterprises use sophisticated business analytics to understand global trends and buying patterns for widgets, to predict customer behavior, and to optimize widget availability and price as a means to maximize revenue growth.

Many companies manage to achieve Level 3, but only sporadically. It is as if they can manage the occasional sprint, but quickly revert to a Level 2 slow jog. They have experienced a digital success or two but are far from being a bona fide digital enterprise which depends upon a high degree of Business-IT maturity and integration.

Business-IT Maturity: Theory of the Case

An analysis of the major drivers behind Business-IT Maturity suggest basic principles for Business-IT evolution such as how IT organizations evolve to capitalize on emerging technologies and enable new and more valuable business models and outcomes.

Level 1 to Level 2	Level 2 to Level 3
Rigor, discipline, standardization	Innovation
Constrain Demand by Supply	Constrain Demand by Business Value
Focus on Project & Service Management	Add Program, Portfolio & Product Management
Establish IT Architecture – bottom up, IT-out	Evolve Enterprise Architecture – top down, business-in
From "Order Taking" to "Service Provider"	From "Service Provider" to "Business Partner"
From "Deliver for the business"	To "Co-create with the business"
Seed with High Performing Individuals	Energize with High Performing Teams & Collaboration
Re-skill though Hiring & Training Events	Up-skill through Continuous Learning & Development

The Business-IT Maturity Journey

Three distinct drivers impact Business-IT Maturity:

1. **Universal Drivers** (inevitable, mostly independent of industry or geography) include:
   - Organizational learning over time
   - Technological evolution
   - Social change (e.g., innovations in consumer use of technology)
   - Global change (e.g., growing awareness of climate change and cyber security)
2. **Business Drivers** include:
   - Changes in the marketplace
   - Competitive threats and opportunities
   - Strategic pressures (e.g., shifts in business strategic intent)
   - Business leadership vision and ambition
   - Putting applications directly in hands of consumers
   - Changes in talent (e.g., talent shortage, shift in workplace demographics, new skills and specialties)
3. **Internal IT Drivers** include:
   - IT leadership vision and ambition
   - Gap between business demand and IT supply capability
   - Competitive threats to internal IT (e.g., outsourcing and cloud computing)
   - IT strategic change (typically in response to business strategic change)

The ways these drivers (especially, the Business and Internal IT drivers) play out for any given company in any industry will shape both business demand and IT supply maturity. IT leadership can either be victims or amplifiers of these drivers.

For example, among the universal drivers, IT leaders can accelerate organizational learning by using IT as an enabler. They can accelerate technological learning by establishing some form of IT technology research lab or by partnering with their strategic suppliers.

IT leaders can accelerate organizational learning by using IT as an enabler

On the other hand, they can become victims of these forces, dooming their enterprises to groundhog days as they relive over and over again chaotic, reactive experiences common to Level 1 Business-IT maturity, or through determination to be slow followers of new technologies.

Understanding these drivers and how well leadership leverages them on the one hand, or becomes a victim to them on the other, might be revealing for assessing the IT maturity trajectory the company is on and identifying how that trajectory must change.

Principles for Increasing Business-IT Maturity

Here are some of the over arching principles for guiding Business-IT maturation. These principles can help accelerate the IT maturity journey and provide guideposts for reaching organizational and structural decisions.

Business-IT Convergence

Business-IT convergence is best understood in the context of Business-IT maturity itself. At low Business-IT maturity, there is a virtual (and sometimes real) wall between the IT organization and the business it serves. As maturity increases, the wall becomes more porous. Roles become quite blended (e.g., business relationship managers and enterprise architects) as IT knowledge is increasingly found in the business, and business knowledge is increasingly found among IT professionals.

> *Business-IT convergence is best understood in the context of Business-IT maturity itself*

At higher levels of Business-IT maturity, IT is a small, highly specialized organization—one that is largely concerned with enterprise architecture and infrastructure. The rest of what most IT organizations do today is dispersed and distributed throughout the business.

Open Source Domination

Open Source makes software code available to all users so it can be modified by any person for any purpose in the collaborative public domain. Open source is increasingly becoming a dominant method for software development.

Public IT Infrastructure Domination (Cloud Computing)

The familiar mantra, the web is the computer has already been established. Over time, few companies will have their own data centers, preferring to use that great on-demand data center in the sky.

The Business-IT Maturity Journey: Reaching Level 3

Level 1 to 2 is internally focused and IT-driven. Getting from L1 to L2 is about bringing order to the chaos, e.g., simplifying IT infrastructure, centralizing control over IT spending and standards, establishing credibility for project results and service performance, implementing strong process disciplines.

Moving from Level 2 to Level 3 requires a flip to an external focus and is business-driven. The L2 to L3 journey is about living with complexity, fostering self-service, decentralizing control and empowering the network. Level 3 Business-IT Maturity is reached when:

- There is no separate IT governance structure. It is converged with business governance.
- There is no separate IT portfolio. It is integrated into the business portfolio.
- There is no separate IT strategy. It is integrated into business strategy.
- There is no separate IT architecture. It is a component of the enterprise architecture.
- There are no separate IT business relationship managers. Relationship management is a widespread and diverse role.

The Level 2 Sticking Points

A major inflexion point comes at the middle of Level 2 Business-IT Maturity. The things organizations have to do to get from Level 1 to Level 2 are quite different from the things organizations must do to get from Level 2 to Level 3. The Business-IT Maturity model is a learning curve and the middle of Level 2 is the steepest part of

> ### Maturity Level 2 Sticking Point: An Example
> *The Level 1 to Level 2 shift typically requires a far more rigorous approach to business cases, often achieved through sophisticated templates and Net Present Value analyses. Now, imagine this Level 3 scenario:*
>
> *A business executive comes in one morning bubbling with an idea she had in the shower about a novel way to incorporate RFID into the company's supply chain. She calls her friendly IT relationship manager and explains the idea. He says, "That's great! Now, here's the business case template. Just figure out the lifecycle costs and value and complete these 12 pages of project definition. The executive, with no idea how to estimate the value of an innovative business capability and daunted by the twelve page template, decides maybe the idea was not that great after all, and drops it!*
>
> *The problem here is that getting from Level 1 to 2 requires a disciplined and consistent approach to framing, prioritizing, and driving transactional solutions. If those same methods are applied to the more innovative possibilities that are the focus for Level 3, they will likely die on the vine. The Level 2 to 3 journey requires more of a portfolio-based approach—portfolio management for all IT investments, and a portfolio of project and program prioritization and approval methods, each suited to the types of investment being considered.*

the curve. Progress at mid-Level 2 can be rapid, but it requires a great deal of focus, energy, and a clear understanding of the steps to be taken and how to take them.

The midpoint on IT Maturity (Level 2) is often a sticking point. IT organizations seem to get stuck there and make little, if any, progress in increasing their maturity. Understanding the causes of these sticking points is important to avoiding them. The midpoint between L2 and L3 is a point of discontinuity. Approximately 70% of businesses in North America are at this point today.

The good news is that progress in that middle space can be fast. The bad news: it is literally an uphill struggle, fraught with ambiguities and elusive shifts in IT's role and direction that IT professionals typically don't like and often are inadequately prepared for.

Consider learning to crawl, then to walk, and then to run. Once a person can crawl, it is no use hoping to walk by trying to crawl faster! It is no good trying to learn to run by walking faster. The movements are different, require different skills and use different muscles.

Similarly, the good and important disciplines introduced at L1, such as consistent

Transformational Change: An Example

I worked with a systems development organization to help them redesign their IT operating model for increased speed and agility. In trying to model the desired end-state behaviors, we moved quickly through a series of highly participative workshops and reached agreement on the design of the new operating model.

The organization's members were (mostly) excited about the changes and eager to get on with it, but they quickly lost momentum as the CIO insisted on more and more detail, financial business cases and so on. He put the leadership team through a lengthy series of monthly reviews.

Nine months later little change had happened. Enthusiasm was waning. The momentum that had been established was gone, and the organization was hoist by its own petard (as the saying goes), as the strong control mindset to prevent bad change squeezed out ambitions for breakthrough creation of good change.

I think one lesson here is reflected in Einstein's belief that we can't solve problems by using the same type of thinking we used when we created them.

> ## The Level 2 Sticking Point
> *Life as a consultant is tough. I'm not complaining, but we have to find small ways to introduce humor and keep our sanity.*
>
> *One of the ways I can put a sparkle into my day is when I meet a CIO I've never met before, at an organization I know nothing about, and after a few minutes into the conversation, I pronounce, "I think your IT funding model is broken!"*
>
> *In every case, they look shocked and then ask, "How did you know so quickly?"*
>
> *Of course, the answer is that funding models are always broken!*

project management, service management and CMMI-based improvement programs that helped an organization get to mid-L2 will not get an organization to L3. The disciplines needed for traditional transactional solutions and applications—the stuff of Level 1 and 2—is not well suited to the focus of Level 3 which demands collaborative, innovative, web-based, and groupware solutions.

Note that in this maturity model, demand is cumulative. Level 1 demand does not go away when an organization gets to Level 2. Level 2 demand continues at Level 3. The processes and disciplines needed to be effective in managing and satisfying the less mature types of demand are important to sustain.

However, in order to stimulate demand for higher level capabilities, and to satisfy that demand, new disciplines must be learned, old ways of doing things must be unlearned, and some older disciplines must be applied with a careful and selective hand.

IT Funding and the Level 2 Sticking Point
One of the more intractable sticking points is in the IT funding model: the ways that IT prices its products and services, and recovers its costs (and, if a profit center, covers its margin). IT funding is one of the dominant causes for sticking at mid-Level 2 Business-IT Maturity. IT funding models are always broken .

At lower maturity, much IT spend is funded by the project. Business clients understand the idea of projects and are usually prepared to fund them if they believe there is a direct benefit to them. They don't really understand IT infrastructure and what it takes to keep it running and positioned for the future.

One of the characteristics of infrastructure is that it is only noticeable when it fails. If infrastructure is working fine, it is invisible except to those who are involved in keeping it working. So IT infrastructure investment requests are typically met by: *"Why do we need to spend $x million moving to Windows version x?"*

Typically at Level 1 maturity, IT infrastructure is funded by some form of allocation or tax. Business leaders don't like this. IT infrastructure always seems to deliver too little and cost too much. IT keeps needing additional spending on mysterious things that should have been anticipated and planned for or avoided.

Level 2 is often about cross-functional systems (ERP, CRM) and support for collaboration and inter-enterprise communications. At Level 2, IT infrastructure becomes an even more significant portion of IT costs. During Level 2, IT is laying down a foundation for shared computing, in effect procuring options for future capability that has not yet been implemented (perhaps not yet defined).

Business executives at Level 2 maturity don't have the IT literacy to appreciate the concepts of infrastructure and options. Costs associated with these things are not easily tied to projects (which clearly have to be funded), and yet stuffing them under the covers as an allocation or tax does nothing to contribute to understanding. It just makes leadership more suspicious and skeptical, questioning whether IT resources are being properly managed.

This leads to the Level 2 trap. IT does not adequately sell the benefits of infrastructure. The business does not adequately understand the value of infrastructure. As a result, IT infrastructure places a drag against progress and slows down increases in Business-IT maturity.

IT Leadership and the Level 2 Sticking Point

Joseph Juran, in his book *Managerial Breakthrough* (1964), distinguished between control and breakthrough. This work is significant because the journey from Level 1 to Level 2 is largely about control while the Level 2 to Level 3 journey is about breakthrough.

> *Although change doesn't always begin at the top, transformational change must ultimately be led from the top*

Although change doesn't always begin at the top, transformational change must ultimately be led from the top. As a result of leading a multi-year longitudinal study of IT organizational transformations, a research team hypothesized that the leadership style and approach needed to transform from Level 1 to Level 2 is quite different from that required to get from Level 2 to Level 3.

When trying to get from Level 2 to Level 3, it is important to look carefully at the leadership and management practices that got the organization to Level 2 and ask: "Will these leaders get the organization to Level 3?"

Some CIOs are better at leading a control-oriented IT organization than others. And some are better at leading organizations that are breakthrough-oriented. CIOs are rarely equally adept at both and are, therefore, rarely capable of leading their IT organizations on the entire journey from Level 1 to Level 3. IT leadership is, of course, about much more than the CIO. The CIO's leadership

The CIO's leadership team, IT managers, and ultimately everyone in the IT organization, have a leadership role

team, IT managers, and ultimately everyone in the IT organization, have a leadership role. However, if the CIO is not bringing the right leadership style and focus to organizational transformation, the leadership team is unlikely to do so.

IT Funding and the Stealth Infrastructure Trap

This is another common sticking point. The logic (or illogic) behind this is: The business does not understand all this infrastructure stuff (or plug in any enterprise-wide IT improvement initiative *du jour*, e.g., Service Oriented Architecture (SOA), enterprise architecture) so other ways to fund it will be found, such as hidden taxes and accounting sleight of hand.

The paradox here is that low maturity businesses do not understand many of the IT infrastructure components. Yet sheltering them from these concepts, denies them the education they need to become more IT literate and more effective in leveraging IT for business value. This is not to suggest that they have to be exposed to the technical minutiae, but they do have to understand the business implications.

Consumers of electric power at home do not need to understand how electrons flow through wire, or how 3-phase electric transmission works, but they do need to understand the risks of ice causing low hanging tree branches to snag transmission lines and potentially cut the power supply when they least need an interruption. An educated consumer is a smart consumer, whether that is a home consumer of electricity, or a corporate consumer of IT.

One method for improving communication is to ensure that individual components are packaged together into bundles that are meaningful to the business partner. Contemporary IT practice is to use the disciplines of service management. The service bundles must make sense to the service consumer and be aggregated at a high enough level to have meaningful business value impact. At the same time they must be sufficiently granular to enable meaningful cost-to-serve/value-of-service trade-offs.

For example, when onboarding a new employee, it is not necessary to negotiate and pay for separate services to equip the employee with a PC, a cell phone, an internet account, passwords, a help desk account, when an *on-boarding new employee service* (one that might well draw from HR databases and other enterprise-wide services bundles) can make on-boarding employees much simpler.

The Unwritten Rules of Business-IT Maturity

The Business-IT Maturity Model addresses Demand maturity (the business appetite for IT enablement) and Supply maturity (the ability to stimulate and satisfy that demand in a safe, secure, predictable, efficient and effective manner). There are unwrit-

Organization Rules

Back in 1994, my esteemed colleague Dr. Peter Scott-Morgan, a leading authority on decoding unwritten rules that define social systems, wrote a remarkable book, The Unwritten Rules of the Game *(1994).*

Having been both a student of and consultant in organizational change, Peter's book crystallized for me many aspects of what we call organizational culture. My ongoing work with Peter, and our research into the hidden logic that drives business performance, helped me expand this understanding and turn that knowledge into practical ways to plan and accelerate organizational change.

Here's the basic idea. All organizations have rules, e.g., don't put unapproved software on your PC. For example:
- *Record your time worked in the official Time Management System.*
- *For projects over 20 hours in duration, follow the formal Project Management methodology*

These rules are known (at least in theory) and are documented. There is an assumption that they will be followed (though the consequences of breaking them is often not clear, and frequently non-existent). There are also a host of unwritten rules. These are equally known (often better known) than the written rules. They have an important impact in driving behaviors.

Unwritten Rules: An Example

One way of thinking about unwritten rules is to imagine the following: A good friend of yours, Bill, is hired into your IT organization. You've known him for years, like him, trust him, and want to see him succeed. What kinds of things would you tell him in his first week at your company?

Here's what you might say: "Bill, it's important here to be actually seen at the monthly town hall meetings. These are webcast to your desktop, but you should try to make it down to the conference center and be seen. Come up with some good questions to ask the CIO in the Q&A session. Try to get on projects sponsored by sales and marketing and stay away from corporate projects. They go on forever and won't help your promotion prospects! Meetings never start on time and always run over, so don't break your neck to get there on time or you'll be sitting around kicking your heels."

I'm sure you can identify many unwritten rules just like these in your own organization. They are powerful drivers of behavior, they are deep seated and, most important, if a change you are trying to introduce is incompatible with the unwritten rules, the unwritten rule must first be replaced with a rule that is more productive.

You can imagine (and have probably seen) the kinds of value-limiting activities and behaviors created by these types of unwritten rule. You may also have seen the kinds of systemic behaviors and vicious cycles that surface from these unwritten rules.

ten rules that impact the supply side and others that impact the demand side.

Given the interdependencies between IT demand and supply, rules on one side that drive dysfunctional behavior frequently impact the other side, often in a vicious cycle. For example: *IT is a necessary overhead cost to be minimized* is a very common demand side unwritten rule that dramatically limits IT performance and business value in an environment that behaves according to such a rule, compared with an organization where the rule is: *IT is a business investment to be leveraged, that can provide significant opportunities for competitive advantage.*

However, if an unwritten rule is predominantly *IT is a cost to be minimized*, business executives won't invest their time and energy in implementing and sustaining the kinds of IT portfolio management and governance that will create real business value—i.e., the unwritten rule becomes a self-fulfilling prophecy, and IT leaders must find a way to modify the unwritten rule and replace it with something more productive.

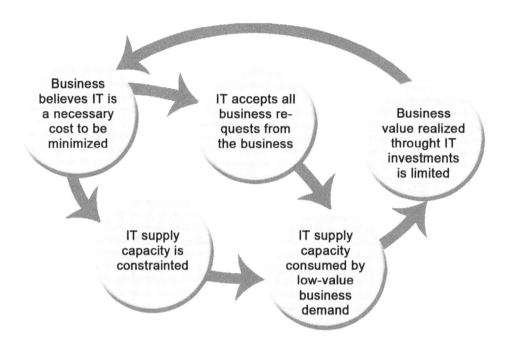

Example Cause-Effect Diagram for the Interactions of Unwritten Rules

Of course, the reality is that IT is both a cost to be minimized and an investment to be leveraged. A good IT portfolio classification scheme helps differentiate between costs that can be minimized and investments that can be leveraged and strong IT portfolio management models and governance practices reinforce the desired behaviors around each investment class.

Another unwritten rule common to Business Demand is, *big systems development initiatives such as ERP implementations are IT projects*. There is also a common unwritten rule on the supply side: *We accept any and all IT requests from the business*.

Today, most enterprises have learned lessons around following these rules and most seasoned CIOs will push back and not collude with such behaviors.

The diagram above shows the combination of the demand side rule: IT is a cost to be minimized (a typical Level 1 and low Level 2 Business-IT maturity rule) and the supply side, all orders are good orders (a typical Level 1 and low Level 2 rule) leads to low value activities being willingly worked by constrained supply resources, yielding low business value from IT investments, and stealing capacity away from potentially higher value opportunities. These dynamics reinforce the sense that IT is a cost to be minimized.

To be effective, IT leaders must be able to surface and understand the unwritten rules that drive both IT demand and supply behaviors and must create interventions (education and awareness building, changes to governance mechanisms, and so forth) to re-shape the unhealthy rules into ones that are value-creative as opposed to value-limiting.

Increasing Maturity by Reducing Complexity

Unwritten rules create characteristics of the Level 1 and low Level 2 Business-IT Maturity that allow (and in some cases caused) the IT environment to become overly complex. With that complexity comes high cost and low agility. This complexity is a sticking point for getting to higher maturity.

Level 1 demand tends to come from individual business units and functions, rather than in support of end-to-end business processes. This is a business maturity as well as IT maturity model and at Level 1, demand tends to be silo-focused, rather than focused on end-to-end business processes.

This siloed demand, coupled with IT's Level 1 order taking supply behavior, is met with siloed supply. The more mature consultative and business partnership-oriented

The Barrier of System and Platform Complexities

Consider a situation where business unit A needs a manufacturing planning system (MRP), as does business unit B, and C, and so on. Soon, you have several MRP systems, all configured differently, often from different vendors, running on different hardware platforms. I had one client who even had trouble producing an accurate count of their MRP systems. They were at mid-Level 2 maturity, and aggressively moving to global common processes and systems. They got to about 47 different systems around the world and gave up trying to count further.

We can imagine the complexity of just maintaining that many different systems, and the resource inefficiencies in doing so. Now imagine adding a data warehousing layer. Think about the data feeds and interfaces that must be built and maintained. Suppose that in Level 2, the business, perhaps forced by market conditions, quality problems, or simply by the need to take out cost, decides to implement lean manufacturing approaches.

The underlying systems and platform complexities become a daunting barrier, typically perceived as an IT problem. Of course in many respects it is an IT problem, unfortunately created by IT's natural response to fragmented business demand.

behaviors tend only to develop at mid-Level 2 and beyond. Also enterprise architecture does not really take hold until mid-Level 2, so all this siloed demand has no overarching business process architecture with which to align.

There are many other aspects to this complexity and the reasons for it. During the early Level 1 stage, COBOL or RPGII might have been the programming language of choice. Later in Level 1, this was supplemented by Fourth Generation Languages such as FOCUS, RAMIS, or MANTIS. Early in Level 2, C++ was the new language of choice, then Java or Python. Each of these *flavor of the month* languages left behind legacy systems, legacy programming and testing tools, and all the other trappings of a development environment that must be maintained.

Below mid-Level 2, the notion of *programs* as opposed to *projects* is not well formed, so there is little sophistication in finding and managing the inter-relationships and dependencies between projects. This adds to the complexity in the legacy environment. There is the complexity of change upon change of technology infrastructure: DOS to Windows to NT to XP Professional, Novell to Microsoft, Microsoft to Open Source, TCAM to VTAM to TCP/IP.

A simple change to one system may result in hundreds of downstream impacts to other systems and interfaces. The changes go on and on. Each change leaves layers of technology and the baggage they imply. In addition, there are the many acquisitions that are never fully integrated.

In some respects, it is deceptively simple for an organization to break out of this com-

Moving to Level 3: A Success Story

Many years ago, I shared an office with a guy who was very structured, probably even anal retentive (as they say). He had a ritual in that if he needed to create a new file, he would always go through the file draw to see what old files could be thrown out. (I'm talking filing cabinets, manila folders and hanging green Pendaflex files!)

One of our only points of frequent tension was that he could not get me to do likewise (I hate throwing stuff away). However, I did see the merit of his obsession, and I see one form of it today as mandatory IT practice. If you are creating something new, you better figure out how you are going to retire stuff that it will (or could or should) replace. This really is a function of IT Process Management, IT Life-cycle Management and IT Portfolio Management.

Moving to Level 3: An Example

How do you break out of this complex environment, leave the boat anchors behind, and move nimbly into Level 3? The answer is in some respects deceptively simple. I'll get to it with a story.

Back in the early 1990s I was running a multi-client research project on IT transformation. One of the big success stories back then (featured in a Harvard Business Review case study) was BP oil. They had grown through acquisition and all the other inevitable sins of Level 1 to the point where their IT infrastructure was exceedingly complex, costly and a constraint on business agility. I was moderating a panel at one of our research workshops.

One of the panelists was a senior BP IT executive, a rather dour Scot with a heavy Scottish brogue. Someone asked him, "How did you deal with all the legacy systems?" He said firmly, in his heaviest Scottish accent, "Och, aye—ya just have to kick it in the teeth!" And with this one line, he really captured the key truth here. You have to have absolute, take no prisoners, executive determination, a just do it approach to change.

He also told us about a giant CDC mainframe dedicated to scientific computing (for analyzing seismic data). The IT leadership team had a strong suspicion that most of the scientific computing had migrated to desktop supercomputers. To prove the point, after several attempts to get people to respond to inquiries about who still needed the CDC machine went nowhere, they simply shut it down, and waited to see who screamed.

One month later, nobody had whimpered, let alone screamed and several million pounds worth of hardware and annual operating costs were promptly decommissioned.

plex environment, leave the boat anchors behind, and move nimbly into Level 3. As described in the story above, an executive determination to *just do it* can be the determining factor.

Weed Pulling and IT Maturity

It is common in many IT shops that processes are heavy on finding, starting, and managing new stuff. However, they are woefully light on stopping, killing or retiring old technology.

It is unfortunate that IT shops have got themselves into a situation where almost all IT resources are consumed maintaining the stuff that's already been built and that this maintenance trap has come as a huge surprise to business and IT leadership. It just kind of crept up on them while they were busy creating.

All IT investments need to be considered in terms of a defined lifecycle with lifecycle costs and benefits estimated, tracked and managed from start to finish. This must become institutionalized behavior for projects, assets, and services. IT processes need explicit steps that address issues related to what can be retired, how can it be retired, how will it be retired.

As an example of best practice, the business case for a new IT investment should not be considered complete until the costs and savings of retirement opportunities associated with the new investment have been considered, and there is another business case triggered for the retirement project (or program).

Creating a Path to Business-IT Maturity

Here are some suggestions for IT leaders who are determined to drive up the business value and impact of Information Technology. Resolve to:

1. *Be more effective in raising awareness of the potential for IT to drive business growth.*
2. *Bring marketing thinking to your IT organization and focus on improving your business communications.*
3. *Innovate IT funding to drive higher business value and more innovative behaviors throughout your enterprise.*
4. *Experiment aggressively with Software as a Service (SaaS).*
5. *Establish the IT organization as the model of collaboration for your enterprise.*
6. *Establish a strong, compelling brand for IT—one known for creating an exceptional customer experience for internal and external partners.*
7. *Significantly strengthen IT talent by looking beyond the traditional recruiting sources and hiring people from entrepreneurial, high tech environments.*
8. *Shift more time and attention from inward-focused activities to looking outside the IT organization to business units, outside the business units to corporate clients and customers, outside the industry to other industries where innovation intensity is significantly higher than in your own.*
9. *Learn more about design thinking and bring more design thinking competence to bear on everything in the IT organization.*
10. *Increase transparency of everything done in IT including communicating from an outside-in perspective in business rather than technology terms.*
11. *Make the IT organization a fun place to work—a place of innovation, experiments and excitement.*

Finally, the proportion of total IT spend consumed by keeping the lights on must be aggressively managed. That means knowing what this proportion is today, defining what it should be in 1 year, 2 years, 3 years, and so on, creating/executing programs and projects to achieve the target portfolio mix, and tracking performance against reaching that target mix.

Professor Peter Weill at the Center for Information Systems Research refers to this as weed pulling. This is a great metaphor and a critical IT discipline.

Retiring Retirement: A Path to Business-IT Maturity

Retiring retirement has become a sensitive issue ever since Ernst & Young completed its landmark research on demographics, culminating in a McKinsey Award-winning

Retiring Retirement as A Path to Business-IT Maturity

I'm increasingly invited to retirement celebrations for former and current consulting clients and friends. They are quite distressing events. First, the retiree is typically putting on a brave face, boasting about all the golf and fishing they will enjoy. But often beneath the surface bluster is a deep-seated fear.

Sometimes they ask me if my firm might have a role for them, or if I know any organizations that could leverage their experience. In spite of the talk of daily golf, they don't want to leave the IT industry, especially now when things seem to be getting more exciting than ever.

These are folks in their early 60s who have been incentivized to take the package. There is an irony as their bosses and peers are often equally fearful of losing access to all the knowledge about to walk out of the door. The dialog goes something like this:

Manager: "Bill's the only one that really understands the manufacturing business and its systems. I don't know how we're going to manage without him!"
VM: "Why don't you create some form of alternate work arrangement for Bill? Perhaps part time?"
Manager: "That would be great, but our company just does not do that kind of thing."

I encourage you to be part of changing these practices at your company and securing for yourself a more reasonable and mutually beneficial trajectory into retirement. I also encourage you to check-in on the website http://www.retire-retirement.com. Look at the white papers and thought pieces available. Buy Tammy Erickson's book, Retire Retirement: Career Strategies for the Boomer Generation, and join the discussions.

Harvard Business Review article and Tammy Erickson's superb book *Retire Retirement: Career Strategies for the Boomer Generation.* (2008).

This book exposes the reader to the issues related to the retirement from industry of an ever increasing number of corporate professionals, and to the very pragmatic, win-win solutions that enlightened firms are now offering. It suggests that IT organizations are often shortchanging themselves by striving to increase Business-IT Maturity while allowing their more mature talent to walk out of the door.

Admittedly there are some old timers who are stuck in the old paradigm. They don't know about things like SOA, SaaS, Enterprise 2.0, and so on, and they don't care to. But there are many professionals who have kept up AND bring the deep knowledge and expertise about their business and systems environment that only comes with fifteen or twenty years in the IT hot seat.

IT Leadership for the Digital Business

Management is necessary, but not sufficient. IT organizations need strong, visionary, and persuasive leaders bound by a shared vision and sense of values

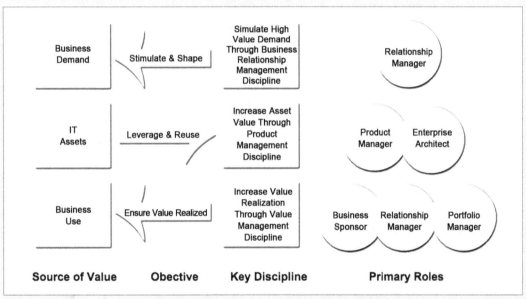

IT Leadership Roles for the Digital Business

Getting from Level 1 to mid-Level 2 Business-IT Maturity is a management challenge. The journey from mid-Level 2 to Level 3 is a leadership challenge.

Overview

This Chapter takes an IT leadership perspective on the future of IT management. It summarizes the impacts upon IT management from the major changes in business, industry, and government. I introduce the concept of Business-IT convergence and the converged IT operating model and drill into optimizing IT capabilities for impact and agility.

IT Leadership for the Digital Business

IT Leadership versus Management

Much has been written about the difference between leadership and management. Leadership is about influencing people through managerial authority (positional power) or without (personal power). Management is about exercising authority.

This basic distinction has important ramifications. Leaders focus on the longer term and typically are concerned with achieving higher levels of performance for their organizations. Managers are more focused on the shorter term, and on achieving agreed upon performance goals.

Great managers often have a hard time transitioning to a leadership role. Great management teams have an even harder time transitioning to leadership teams where team members mutually reinforce each other's instinct to be directive and focus on details.

Observing behaviors, especially in formal meeting settings, is usually very telling about the leadership/management balance. Many senior IT leaders would agree that their leadership teams need to schedule time to talk about strategic issues. Most weekly IT leadership team meetings tend to be consumed by tactical and operational topics.

When an IT leadership team is consumed by tactical and operational details, it is not a leadership team. It is a management team—which is a very different beast. IT processes and management systems should take care of most things so that management of tactical and operational issues can be on auto-pilot. If IT Leadership needs to be a management team, then it is colluding with the dysfunctional behaviors of the managers under them, which is a very unhealthy state.

IT Management vs. Leadership: An Example

I once worked with the CIO and his team at a major financial services company. They had been through a multi-year transformation under their new CIO. The CIO and his team had been hands on and directive. The results had been positive, and the business partners of IT were impressed by the gains made from the transformation.

But like many transformations I have seen, their performance improvement efforts had plateaued. Managers and workers in the IT organization felt dis-empowered, so there was no real culture of continuous improvement. The results of the annual engagement survey showed significantly lower employee engagement in IT than anywhere else in the company.

I raised the subject at an IT leadership team meeting by posing the question: "Are you a leadership team? Or a management team?"

Consensus was quickly reached that they were a management team, with this finding justified by the sorry state of IT prior to transformation, and the need for the top people in IT to drive change.

I asked that IT team, "What do you need to be now, a management or a leadership team?"

This turned out to be contentious, especially as we drilled into what behavioral shifts would be implied if they did shift into a true leadership role. For example, could they really trust their IT managers to manage? If not, would they replace them with those they did trust to manage? Dealing with this question and its implications became a major theme of my work with that team for the balance of the consulting engagement.

Preparing for a New Era of IT Leadership

If history is any indicator, the natural behavior of IT managers is to be very conservative in their approach to emerging technologies. They often tend to be blind to (or at least, choose to ignore) the trends and drivers going on around them in the interests of protecting the enterprise and keeping its assets safe.

Of course, there are notable exceptions where IT leadership is embracing new opportunities and limitations, or at least trying to understand the options. While there will always be important roles for technology experts, since information and IT permeate every aspect of business, industry, and government, leadership roles are going to belong to those who:
* Can connect the dots from business outcomes to technology enablers
* Skillfully surface and shape business demand for information and IT

- Orchestrate resources to meet that demand
- Truly understand how to turn information and IT into tangible, realized business value
- Are passionate about sharing their knowledge for the common good, rather than positioning themselves as the experts and high priests of the IT profession
- Are as passionate about business success and innovation as they are about IT

IT Leadership: Caught Between Two Realities

Being an IT leader is always challenging. The *career is over* distortion of the CIO acronym is humorous because of the real-world challenges associated with the CIO job. Today is an especially challenging time for IT leaders because these jobs are typically

---

IT Reality 1.0

- *IT must be managed. It is difficult, complex, and fraught with crucial technical details. Mastering these details requires teams of technical experts following rigorous processes and procedures. Issues that non-technical people don't often think about — such as backup and recovery, security and privacy, regulatory compliance, business continuity — must be planned for, and managed by, IT specialists who have been properly trained and certified in these disciplines.*
- *IT should be owned and must be controlled internally. IT holds that business users must be protected from themselves, and from the outside world.*
- *Qualified IT resources are scarce and costly. They take time to develop and cannot be ramped up or down quickly. Therefore, long term planning and concerns about scaling are constantly on the IT professional's mind.*
- *IT is obsessed with risk avoidance. Constantly aware of many of the horror stories that are told around the IT campfires (and sometimes involved in either perpetrating or recovering from such horrors), IT leaders work to prevent the many risks associated with IT.*
- *IT deploys sophisticated tools and governance processes to filter the many opportunities for IT-enablement, and weed out all but the key initiatives that justify the investment and risks.*
- *IT perceives the world of IT as relatively closed and proprietary. Therefore, IT is obsessed with IT architectures and standards, and with figuring out how to weave together point solutions into capabilities that meet enterprise needs.*
- *IT is about large projects and solutions such as multi-month, (sometimes multi-year) initiatives designed to last for years.*
- *IT separates the world into development and production. The move from one to the other is like the move through an airlock from a dangerous and polluted free-for-all space into the safe, secure, and sterile data center.*

---

caught somewhere between two very different realities—IT Reality 1.0 (on the previous page) and IT Reality 2.0 (below).

IT Reality 2.0
- *IT is simple, ubiquitous, and inherently safe.*
- *Almost anyone can be creative and productive with IT. All they need is an internet connection and a device equipped with a web browser.*
- *If the user knows nothing, they can simply leverage what is already on the web and learn as they do so. If they know a little and are adventurous, they can do much more than passively leverage what is already there. They can mash up new capabilities from existing ones to solve new problems. They can learn as they go, become even more adventurous and creative, and perhaps even commercialize what they have created. Over time they will become even more skilled, creating more sophisticated solutions, or leveraging crowdsourcing to engage others to help them create the solutions they need.*
- *IT does not care about IT ownership or control. IT cares about results.*
- *IT views the world as a sea of opportunities and solutions to be tried and exploited.*
- *IT sees IT resources as ubiquitous, found with a click of the mouse, engaged with a few more clicks, and paid only when they've delivered. There are no long-term commitments or overhead payments to worry about or justify.*
- *IT is about risk management, moving incrementally, and organically managing risks as they are recognized.*
- *IT has no time for bureaucratic processes such as governance committees and cost justification hoops to run through.*
- *IT sees any opportunity as worthy of a quick experiment to see if its real. It believes that in the time it takes to create a business case or wait for the next governance committee meeting, the idea can be tested and validated, or eliminated. Let the proof of the pudding be in the eating (so to speak), not in the political machinations of investment review bodies.*
- *IT perceives the world of IT as essentially open. Things in its world naturally fit together. Therefore, things can be built in small incremental steps, evolving in the light of experience and changing needs. Things can also be built as discrete point solutions and that can be fitted together if need be.*
- *IT is about small projects and solutions with big impact created in days or weeks and designed for just as long as they are effective.*
- *IT views development and production as living side-by-side in some virtual place in the sky. While IT is working on a solution, it is in development. Once solutions are working, IT declares them in production.*

From Alignment to Convergence

I posted on this topic back in 2009 and would never have dreamed of returning to it if it had not been for a flurry of responses to a conversation someone started on a LinkedIn group. The conversation began with this question: What can IT do to better align itself with the needs of the business?

Responses were all over the map. Some were thoughtful, some trite, some tongue in cheek, others dismissive. Others became argumentative. Most were motherhood and apple pie. They were hard to fault, but not very insightful or helpful. Few of them, if any, added anything new. Some shared my view that the whole notion of alignment was way past its sell-by date.

A CIO still struggling to achieve alignment has not only missed that boat but has failed to recognize that for those who must cover great distances, boat travel was replaced by jet travel years ago (to push the transportation metaphor further.) As one CIO noted: That type of Business-IT alignment thinking went away many years ago. IT, like all other disciplines, is part of the business. It is integrated into it.

When is the last time you heard that manufacturing, accounting, marketing, distribution, or clinical care is aligned with the business? They are the business, and IT is embedded into each and every one of them.

The big challenge is that today's IT reality is neither 1.0 or 2.0. It is in transition. Author William Gibson accurately summarized this when he observed that *the future is already here, but right now it is unevenly distributed*. This uneven distribution of IT realities presents both a curse and an opportunity to IT leaders. For the progressive leadership, this is a wonderful opportunity to shift IT into overdrive. For the late adopters, this is going to make their lives increasingly more miserable.

Shifting From Alignment to Convergence

While it is easy to object to the we/they language that positions IT as something separate from the business, and while it is interesting to ponder what it means to integrate IT into the business, IT covers too much territory to be a useful unit of analysis.

Rather than bundle all IT-related activities under one grand acronym, evaluating the nature of Business-IT convergence becomes much more manageable when it is described in terms of a handful of IT capabilities (for example seven to nine). For this reason, it is important to deconstruct IT into major components (as shown in the graphic on the following page).

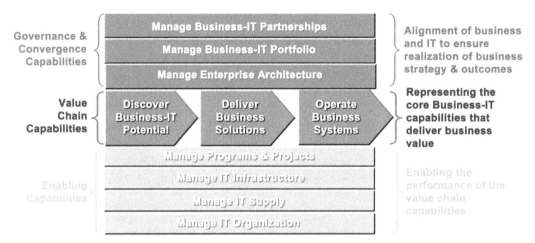

Governance & Convergence, Value Chain, and Enabling Capabilities

Architecting and operating a shared IT infrastructure (networks, data centers, etc.) is quite different from discovering new opportunities to innovate a business model. Protecting information security and integrity is very different from re-engineering a business process to improve the customer experience.

Some of these capabilities (conceiving business value solutions, for example) clearly belong embedded in the *business of the business*. Others (e.g., managed infrastructure and services) are best managed by specialists and shared across business units and processes as reliable, predictable, and well-managed services.

Business Relationship Management

Key to integrating business and IT is the role, discipline, and organizational capability of Business Relationship Management (BRM). The concept of BRM is related to (and employs) many of the techniques and disciplines of customer relationship management (CRM). However, while CRM most often refers to the external customers of a company, Business Relationship Management typically deals with internal customers and business partners.

According to the Business Relationship Management Institute definition, BRM stimulates, surfaces, and shapes business demand for IT services and capabilities, and ensures that the potential business value is captured, optimized, and recognized.

If it sometimes feels like there is a wall between the IT organization and the business it serves, BRM represents a perfectly transparent window in that wall:

- An opening through which the IT organization becomes part of the business it services, and the business becomes part of the IT organization serving it
- An opening that translates business-speak into IT-speak and vice versa
- An opening that allows the IT professionals to become business savvy, and the business professionals to become IT savvy
- An opening through which business and IT integrate or converge over time

Looking at Web 2.0 through the lens of waiting for business problems to appear, falls short of leveraging powerful opportunities. These types of technologies, almost by definition, drive opportunity from the outside in, and from the bottom or middle up.

The New IT Role: From Problem Solving to Opportunity Creation
IT management consulting has changed over the years. The changes for IT management consulting in many ways mirror the changes in the role of IT, at least as far as the more mature Business-IT environments are concerned.

Problem Solving vs Opportunity Identification
Think about your own relationships with the plumber or car repair shop compared to those with a primary physician. I don't care how little the plumber knows about me as a person. I just want the leak fixed quickly, without getting ripped off. But I do want my doctor to know enough about me to guide me in managing my health. Consider some of the differences between problem solving and opportunity finding:

- *Problems tend to be brought to you (to map back to the IT management consulting analogy, the problems often come to you via a request for proposal), whereas you have to go and look for opportunities.*
- *When people bring you problems to solve, they are hoping for a solution. When you find an opportunity, you might have a very hard time selling your business partner on something they weren't looking for in the first place and that does not solve a recognized problem.*
- *The tools used for problem solving are quite different from those used for opportunity identification. You might be a master black belt in quality improvement, but not know how to innovate or the principles of design thinking.*
- *The solutions available for problem solving are often off-the-shelf while those required to exploit new opportunities may need to be either invented or mashed up from component pieces.*
- *The skills needed for problem solving (e.g., analysis, design) are different from those required for opportunity creation (e.g., synthesis, innovation, persuasion).*
- *The relationships involved in problem solving are quite different from those involved in opportunity identification.*

Business Problem or Business Opportunity?

I had an interesting conversation with a consulting client. The CIO had a strong sense that Web 2.0 was going to be important to the business and, therefore, to the IT organization. He couldn't put his finger on why, what it all means, and what to do about it, but his instincts told him it was too important to ignore, so he invested time, effort, and some money pulling his top IT leaders together for an off-site to raise awareness and explore options and possibilities. I was invited to facilitate the session.

One IT leader raised the question, "What is the business problem we are trying to solve here?" (The CIO was not present for this interchange.) Several of the other IT leaders latched onto this with a general consensus that there was no particular business problem to be solved and therefore the topic of Web 2.0, while interesting, was not especially relevant and certainly not urgent. Given that everyone was busy, it was probably best to declare the off-site event a success and move on.

This misses a crucial point. One way of thinking about the progression of business demand maturity, and the corresponding progression of IT supply maturity, is that:

- *Level 1 is about improving business efficiency. In other words, Level 1 is about enabling the business*
- *Level 2 is about improving business effectiveness . Level 2 is about solving business problems*
- *Level 3 is about innovating the business. Level 3 is about finding business opportunities*

These homilies can sound trite and simplistic, but I strongly believe that underneath these simple-minded expressions are some important truths. If you look at Web 2.0 through the lens of waiting for business problems to appear, you will probably fall short in leveraging powerful opportunities. I'm convinced that these types of technologies, almost by definition, drive opportunity from the outside-in, and from the bottom-up.

The goal is to facilitate technology use, empower technology users, and watch carefully to see what happens. This is a very different paradigm from the traditional IT world of business enablement or business problem solving. There is no business problem here. There is a business opportunity.

Like the nature/nurture arguments, there is no simple answer. A greater energy and a more powerful sense of outcome surrounds proactive innovators compared to reactive controllers.

For many years, IT specialists inside large businesses and agencies (excluding companies whose business is primarily IT) have pursued a role of problem solver.

- Too much slack in the supply chain? Problem solved. IT can help re-engineer business process, and enable the supply chain with slick supply chain software.
- Too hard to make meaning out of all the transaction data that gets generated every day? Problem solved. IT can build a data warehouse and provide sophisticated data analytics to help the business make better, more informed decisions.
- Have any other problems? Problem solved. The IT organization will help analyze them, determine root causes, then design and implement solutions.

IT as problem solver has been a worthy role for years. The results, more often than not, have been successful. Note how similar this is to the role of the IT management

A Tale of 2 CIOs: Proactive Innovator vs. Reactive Operator

In 2007, in the midst of the great recession, I had the privilege of participating as a speaker and moderator at a joint IT/HR Summit on Next Generation Technologies for Next Generation Enterprises. This was a 3-day session where CIOs and VPs of HR came together to share and learn about key business issues on their joint agendas.

It truly was a privilege to be part of this event which included presentations by Professor Andrew McAfee (Harvard Business School), Don Tapscott (Executive Chairman, Blockchain Research Institute), Professor David Ulrich (University of Michigan, author of Human Resource Champions *(1996)), Tammy Erickson (Tammy Erickson Associates) and yours truly. I got a lot out of the speaker sessions, but also found the dialog and networking to be highly stimulating and informative. Inevitably, many of the conversations steered to the global economy and the role of IT leadership in a recessionary climate.*

I found two sharply divided world views among the many engaging CIO and VP HR conversations. With some poetic license, I represent those opposing world views on page 48. Cecil Controller and Ivan Innovator represent the extremes—most of the CIOs I spoke to at the event were closer to a middle ground. But examining the extremes may stimulate your own thinking about this issue. What do you believe is the proper role of IT leadership today?

I find it interesting to think about the drivers of these opposing views. Are some CIOs inherently more optimistic, and therefore proactive? Or is it the company and its leadership that sets the tone—either empowering the optimists to grow and innovate their way out of a recession, or scaring the pessimists to step into the shadows and idle till the clouds pass by?

Views of Ivan Innovator and Cecil Controller on Recessions

Cecil Controller

Economic conditions spell a period of retrenchment for IT. IT leadership has to take out costs to help the business weather the downturn. As such, many of the initiatives that were planned or started are being put on hold. This is hunkering down time. No one knows how long it will last, but the industry analysts are betting at least a year. Optics are all important here. IT needs to show its business partners that IT understands the economic climate, and that this is a time for IT to take a low profile, cut back its spending, and do its part to help the company weather the down market.

Ivan Innovator

A recession is a time for the IT function to shine by showing leadership and fostering innovation. To do that, and to buy themselves business credibility and IT bandwidth, IT leaders have to aggressively cut costs. They also need to shift IT resources from low to higher value activity. Cost cutting actions are something they have wanted to do for some time, but now the economic climate provides the needed air cover.

The value proposition to the business is double-edged: IT is going to aggressively retire IT systems and assets that are no longer critical to running or growing the business. IT will then redirect the resources that are freed up by the rationalization and consolidation of technology platforms, and focus them on more innovative and higher value initiatives.

The other side of this is that the business partners of IT have never needed IT to focus on growth and innovation more than they do in these financially austere times. There has been a sea change in available technologies, and IT leadership has to find value-producing ways to tap these new technologies. If the IT and the business can beat its competitors to the punch, the company can turn the economic climate to its advantage. And that is the focus of IT.

---

consultant. For years IT management consultants have been brought in when there is a problem the CIO needs help solving. But over the last few years, IT dependency on consultants has been changing.

Most of the traditional IT management problems have been solved, or at least the CIO's team and their business partners have solved similar problems before, and feel qualified to solve them internally without calling on outside resources for assistance.

The big problems have either been solved, or the tools and disciplines of 6 Sigma, business process re-engineering, and other problem-solving methods are now reasonably

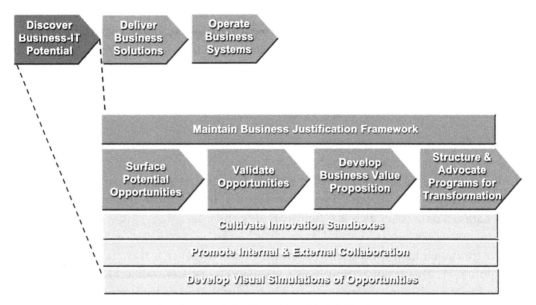

An Approach to Operating Model Design

well known, and have become relatively routine. So it may be instructive to explore the future role of IT professionals in this changing environment.

The cutting edge of IT today—with Web 2.0, cloud computing, and the evolving convergence between the consumer space and enterprise computing—has shifted the paradigm for the IT professional from problem solving to opportunity identification and exploitation.

This may seem like a subtle, semantic shift, but it is a shift that is profound because it impacts the competencies IT pros need to be successful, and the way they see and operationalize their role and their relationships with their business partners.

Creating a Business-IT Converged Operating Model

Business-IT convergence is a consequence of the evolution of IT, which is simultaneously becoming:

- **More ubiquitous.** Towards the end of the 20th Century, IT helped transform information intensive industries (e.g., financial services), but in the 21st Century, the transformational power of IT is just about everywhere, from sports, to industry, to government, and to communities and social networks.
- **More accessible.** With the consumerization of IT, powerful mobile computing, and readily available cloud-based services, just about everyone has access to potent

technology capabilities.

- **More capable.** Touch screens, voice commands, location-based services, cheap data storage, and the ability to analyze all types of information across multiple sources, give people worldwide access to computing resources that were previously only available to the largest, most sophisticated companies and government agencies.

Business-IT convergence shows up in many ways. The consumerization of IT, where the line between corporate and personal technology is blurring, is an aspect of convergence. Employees now expect to be able to use the same technologies at home and at the office. They expect the search for information to be as simple and rapid across their organization's data bases as it is when searching the internet.

A more fundamental implication of Business-IT convergence is the changing nature of corporate IT. This is not as simple as a reversion to a decentralized IT organization. Rather, Business-IT convergence occurs when roles that were traditionally embedded in the IT organization are now formally embedded in the business.

This has major implications for IT infrastructure, the stuff that must be efficiently, reliably, safely, and cost-effectively shared across the enterprise. It also has implications for what moves to the cloud, what types of cloud service should be used, and whether to transition off existing enterprise application platforms.

Creating a Business-IT Converged Operating Model: An Example

I was introduced to the phenomenon of Business-IT convergence in the late 1980s by one of the world's leading IT thinkers and teachers—Professor James Cash (then Professor and Senior Associate Dean at Harvard Business School and a board member for Microsoft, GE, State Street Bank, and Walmart).

I had just delivered a presentation about Business-IT alignment to an audience of CIOs. The presentation was well received, and I was initially thrilled when Professor Cash approached me and said he found my presentation interesting. The expression, damned with faint praise, came to mind, but this led to a conversation about convergence being a more effective approach to closing the Business-IT chasm than alignment had proven to be.

I subsequently had the opportunity to work with and learn from Jim Cash during the early 1990s as we collaborated on IT management research, IT leadership and Business Relationship Management development.

The Changing Nature of the IT Organization

With these changes, the days when there were two types of IT people—IT professionals and IT end users—are quickly passing. Today there are end users who have access to tools that let them accomplish more with IT in an hour than could be accomplished by yesterday's IT professionals in a week.

The days when there were two types of IT people—IT professionals and IT end users—are quickly passing

There are people who would be considered IT professionals in every respect, except one. They don't work for an IT organization. Rather, they are deeply embedded in the business. The distinction between staff and line has changed dramatically.

Shadow IT—where technology is purchased and managed by end users, not IT—is no longer an aberration to be eliminated. It is becoming the norm, with the traditional corporate IT organization becoming the shadow.

As predicted by Alvin Toffler in *The Third Wave* (1980), the artificial gap between producer and consumer is being healed, giving rise to the IT *prosumer* and to Business-IT convergence.

Three Dimensions of Value Realization

Three dimensions of value realization are important to driving business value. They are shown in the graphic at the beginning of this Chapter (p. 37), and are described in more detail below. These drivers include:

1. Shaping business demand
2. Leveraging IT assets and information
3. Optimizing business use

Shaping Business Demand

At low maturity, an IT organization is often referred to as *order takers* for business requests. On the face of it, this sounds customer-centric and responsive. The reality is that, at low maturity, business demand yields relatively little business value.

It is also the case that when the business partner has already figured out what they need before they engage IT (or if the business partner is depending on external consultants and vendors to tell them what they need), then the opportunities for the IT organization to add value become very limited.

If an IT organization is able to engage with their business partners earlier—to be proactive, not simply responsive—they can stimulate, surface, and shape demand towards higher value opportunities. These high value opportunities tend to suppress demand for low value activities, with the result that more people are working on high value opportunities.

Shaping business demand is an important discipline for increasing IT maturity and, with it, driving more value from IT.

> *Shaping business demand is an important discipline for increasing IT maturity and driving more value from IT*

Associated with this discipline is the role of Business Relationship Manager (BRM). This role sits between an IT organization and its business partners. In leading practice organizations, the BRM role (by any title) is focused on demand management with an eye to elevating business value of IT.

Leveraging IT Assets and Information

At low IT maturity, much effort goes towards establishing a supportive, reliable, and predictable infrastructure, and the business applications that depend upon that infrastructure. Typically, these business applications go significantly under-leveraged. The cost, effort, and business disruption associated with their deployment tends to contribute to a mentality of *declare success and move on.*

Business users need time to catch their breath. They also need to be shown new ways to leverage the platforms and the mountains of information they generate. Also, while IT organizations typically do a good job maintaining these business applications, there is no single role focused on managing their total lifetime value.

To increase maturity, architectural and asset management disciplines must be established around business applications, so as to create business platforms and products that enable business process improvement and innovation. Platforms—such as the iPhone as a platform, with open, published application programming interfaces (API), the Apple Store, and thousands of apps available to run on that platform—are inherently extensible and readily leveraged.

The role responsible for these architectural and asset management disciplines is referred to as product management. Product management is an important aspect of reaching higher maturity and driving business value, thereby ensuring that the full potential value of business platforms and products is exploited and harvested. The BRM role works closely with product managers to help create the business appetite for new business capability that leverages the underlying business platforms and products.

Optimizing Business Use

Low maturity IT organizations focus on building, implementing, and maintaining business solutions. As maturity increases, the focus expands to help optimize the business value realized though the use of technology solutions. Optimization depends upon the discipline of value management. This, in turn, leverages competencies in business change management and portfolio management.

Key IT Roles for Driving Business Value

As the nature of IT changes, roles that were formerly the domain of the IT professional and that existed as part of an enterprise IT organization are migrating into the business line organization. An example of this migration is shown in the graphic on p. 37.

As the nature of IT changes, roles that were formerly the domain of the IT professional are migrating into the business

Simultaneously, roles that were deeply embedded in the business (even if they were cloaked in shadows) are being assumed by professional IT. Four roles are associated with these shifting disciplines:

- Business sponsor for a given initiative
- Portfolio manager
- Business change consultant
- BRM with its focus on demand management and business value realization

These are IT roles, not jobs. A role is not the same thing as a job. For example, business architect, process specialists, and information analyst are roles that are often embedded in the business, but that are not necessarily job titles. A role is like a hat worn by an individual who meets certain qualifications (possess certain competencies). A person qualified to wear a specific hat has certain responsibilities and accountabilities. Some people will fill multiple roles, depending upon circumstances and needs.

Roles, the competencies they demand, the processes in which they participate, and the ways they engage with other roles, are all characteristics that are defined in an IT operating model.

Optimizing IT Capabilities for Business Value

In their ground breaking book, *The Discipline of Market Leaders* (1997), coauthors Michael Tracy and Fred Wiersema argue that companies that have taken leadership positions in their industries have typically done so by focusing their strategy on one of three value disciplines, and by optimizing their business operating models accordingly.

In choosing one discipline to focus attention on, leaders don't ignore the other two value disciplines. They meet industry standards in all three disciplines, but they lead in, and optimize for, one of the three value disciplines (as shown below):

- **Operational excellence.** Customer proposition is process-centric, offering lowest price, hassle-free service
- **Product leadership.** Customer proposition is knowledge centric, offering products and services that push performance boundaries
- **Customer intimacy.** Customer proposition is customer centric, anticipating customer needs delivering what specific customers want

Thinking of an internal IT organization in business terms, it becomes clear that IT infrastructure and operations are optimized for operational excellence, and that enterprise architecture and solutions delivery should be optimized for product leadership.

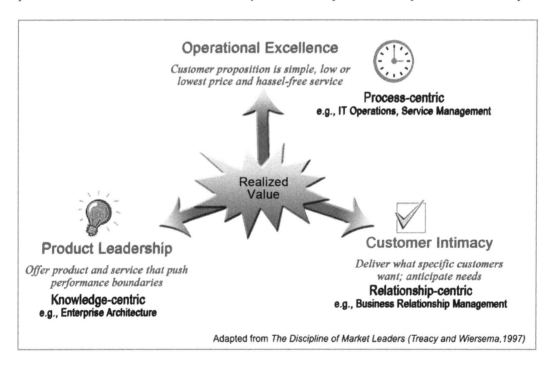

The open question is: How can IT best optimize for customer intimacy?

Achieving Customer Intimacy

Many years ago (and even today in some companies) business leaders achieved customer intimacy with their IT capabilities by establishing their own dedicated IT organizations.

Over the years, as IT became an increasingly larger share of business budgets, IT organizations evolved to gain advantages of scale by consolidating IT capabilities into centralized shared service organizations. These tended to be optimized for operational excellence, consistent with the lowest price and hassle-free service promise associated with the business case for centralization.

For many centralized shared service IT capabilities, the customer intimacy value discipline is lost under the pressure to take out cost and be operationally excellent. The business partners of the IT organization can have anything they want as long as their requirements are consistent with the enterprise IT infrastructure, and draw from the portfolio of standard enterprise solutions. In other words, anything goes as long as one size fits all.

The irony of the situation is that at the same time business leaders attempt to be more

BRM and Operational Excellence

In today's leading IT organizations, the customer intimacy value discipline is being restored through the emerging role of Business Relationship Manager (BRM) charged with driving business value from information and IT by getting close to their internal (and external) customers. According to Treacy and Wiersema, this happens by delivering what specific customers want and by anticipating what customers need.

This approach works as long as IT infrastructure and operations live up to the operational excellence value discipline. When operational excellence is lacking, internal customers are typically reluctant to engage their BRMs in strategic exploration while basic operational issues (metaphorically keeping lights on and trains running on time) are disrupting business operations.

When BRMs get sucked into operational issues, their role is inconsistent with the main mission of Business Relationship Management. Solving operational issues might feel good, heroic even, but it is not what the BRM role is about. Operational issues should be solved in those organizational entities that are charged with, and optimized for, operational excellence.

competitive and get closer to their customers, IT organizations, in the name of defensible cost structures, move further away from their customers.

Enter the Business Relationship Manager

With many BRMs transitioning into their role from other IT disciplines, including service management and project management, there is often a strong temptation to step up to the plate, and compensate for the deficiencies in operational excellence.

There are several traps inherent in this strategy:

1. When BRMs step into an operational excellence role, they are taking time and energy away from their customer intimacy role. They tend to become part of the problem their role was established to address.
2. When the business partner sees the BRM in an operational excellence role, the BRM may have a hard time establishing or sustaining a relationship based upon strategic insight.
3. By masking operational issues, the BRM is essentially colluding with dysfunctional behavior, and potentially weakening opportunities for operational improvement.

An Effective Approach for Addressing Operational Issues

Rather than fall into the collusion trap, effective BRMs leverage their influence, their persuasion skills, and their competencies in organizational change management by stepping into the role of change agent for improved IT operations and infrastructure.

They fearlessly call out process issues by:

1. **Gathering and presenting data** that highlights process issues and their implications, always focusing on the process rather than the people
2. **Offering to help fix process issues** by volunteering their business customer perspective, facilitation and process management skills, organizational change management capabilities, and any other competencies they can bring to the table
3. **Creating synergistic foxholes with their IT colleagues** by establishing (or reinforcing) shared goals, common enemies (such as poor process, rework, dissatisfied business customers), and mutual dependencies

Managing IT in a Digital Enterprise

4

The high priests and priestesses of IT are no longer the only source of IT talent

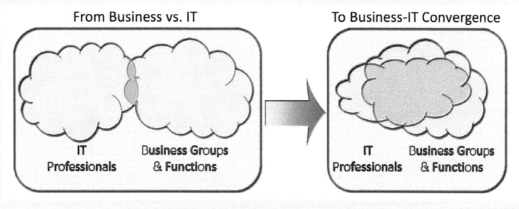

Shift From Centralized or Distributed IT to Dispersed IT

IT needs to help service consumers be smart, knowledgeable, and largely self-sufficient.

Overview

This Chapter considers ways to manage IT transition as we move further into the digital enterprise. It looks at ways to digitize the IT operating model and when to take an incremental or revolutionary approach. It examines the requirements and characteristics of a digital enterprise IT operating model and how the lens of chaos theory and capabilities such as cloud computing can inform and accelerate IT transformation approaches.

Managing IT in a Digital Enterprise

IT On-demand

A common theme for the emerging digital enterprise is IT on-demand. This idea gets interpreted in different ways, often purloined as a *marketing buzz*, but implies the ability to access a service where it is wanted, when it is wanted, and how it is wanted. This is a level of service that is both powerful and, ultimately, game changing for IT management.

On-demand connotes speed, agility, flexibility, customization, and personalization. It need not connote armies of IT professionals sitting in the wings waiting, ready to perform when required. That might be one way to manage the capacity issue but clearly, it is not an economically viable or sustainable approach.

Rather, IT on-demand connotes an IT capability that demonstrates mastery in global sourcing, and has created an enabling architecture where services are readily identified, found, and leveraged—whether at a granular level, or at a richer *mashup level* where basic services are aggregated into higher capability services and solutions.

IT on-demand has implications both for the supply of services and for the service consumer who must become a collaborator in the new world of on-demand services. For digital enterprise IT capability, the most significant roles become relationship and business value management, service provisioning, service architecting, and helping service consumers become smart and skillful at service consumption.

On-demand services must be architected from the perspective of the service user. They must be easy to find, easy to use, and designed to work for consumers when, where, and how they want. To offer service consumers this range of services on-demand,

> ## Future Vision of 2017 (circa 2007)
> *When I started my blog in 2007, my vision of IT circa 2017 was that in the future there would be much more formality, sophistication, and discipline around the IT infrastructure capability, with much higher reliance on open, public infrastructures. All of which would be coordinated the way an effective procurement function works.*
>
> *At the same time, most of the other traditionally IT roles (e.g., demand management, business innovation, product management) would be liberally dispersed deep inside business units, often associated with specific business process-oriented roles.*

there must be a strong element of self-service, and the information and incentives consumers need to decide the level of service they need, and how they need it.

This is the type of IT operating model that the digital enterprise IT capability must prepare and design for. IT services need to help service consumers be smart, knowledgeable, and largely self-sufficient. This is an important shift from doing more for the customer to helping them achieve more value. In the digital enterprise, IT organizations become more like infrastructure.

Why Web 2.0 Will Render Today's IT Organization Obsolete
There are two major reasons that today's IT organization model will become obsolete over the next dozen years or so.

1. Just as the PC democratized computing, Web 2.0 is revolutionizing it in a far-reaching way. The PC moved computing from the mainframe glasshouse to the desktop, and ultimately to the laptop and smart phone. Web 2.0 is moving computing (and nearly all the associated software needed to compute) from the desktop/laptop to the cloud. As mentioned in Chapter 1, when the PC first appeared, even a modest tool, such as Visicalc, had non-IT professionals doing things with computers that would have taken some pretty heavy-duty Fortran programmers to achieve. Today, end users are doing things with mashups and widgets that would have required experienced web programmers to achieve just a couple of years ago.

2. IT professionals, and the organizations they staff, are not just providers of IT products and services. They are also consumers. As such, they too will benefit from Web 2.0 (although they may not be the first to the party.) The type of collaborative capabilities needed by today's enterprises lend themselves to collaborative IT management approaches. Think of it this way, virtually everyone will be a programmer, system administrators will be everywhere, and technical specialists will be ubiquitous.

Although this may be taking an extreme position, and the reality will be somewhat less severe, for many, collaborative IT has great potential to remedy some of the shortcomings of the typical IT organization.

The Flawed Notion of an IT Organization

Business-IT alignment has been an on-going challenge since the introduction of data processing, always showing up at or near the top of biggest issues lists in annual computer magazine surveys. Having an IT organization that translates business requirements into IT specifications and solutions is, at best, a flawed approach.

There is always an aspect of the IT organization that adds cost but not value. This is inherent in the role of intermediaries. If the business needs a translator, something will always get lost in translation. How can business tell IT what it wants when the busi-

Future Vision of 2020 (circa 1980)

I first read Alvin Toffler's remarkable book, The Third Wave *(1980) in 1980. In that book Toffler pointed out that the separation between production and consumption is not the natural order of things. It occurred to me at that time that the need for an IT organization represented an unnatural separation of IT consumption from production. I came to realize that the whole notion of the IT organization, especially as it was typically configured in the 1980s, was essentially a temporary phenomenon.*

In retrospect it's worth noting the IT context around 1980. Apple had introduced the Apple II in 1977 and IBM legitimized personal computing as an enterprise capability with its introduction of the IBM PC in 1981. Suddenly Toffler's words as they applied to enterprise IT appeared prophetic. Nearly 40 years later, having conducted literally dozens of global multi-company research programs examining various facets of IT effectiveness and having worked with hundreds of IT organizations over much of the world, I am more convinced than ever that no IT organization is good enough for the institutions that they support or able to fully leverage the incredible emerging power of IT.

For millennia, human beings as individuals, families and small communities produced what they needed to consume. This worked well until the Industrial Revolution when separation of production from consumption became necessary to fuel the industrial age (which Toffler called the Second Wave). With the industrial revolution there was a breach (as Toffler referred to it) between production and consumption. It was an unnatural act that would be healed over time by technology. Fast forward 40 years to the age of mass collaboration, mass customization, crowdsourcing, open source and Wikinomics. Toffler's words ring true today to a degree unimaginable back then.

ness doesn't know what it wants until it sees it?

The internet has *disintermediated* many types of services by increasing pricing transparency, and by eliminating (or at least reducing) supply/demand asymmetries. The internet has also led to new forms of intermediation (such as aggregators, brokers, agents), but these are not of the same type as those that were disintermediated.

The alternative in the era of Web 2.0 is to give business the right tools, and allow it to explore and play. The business will discover what they want and need to satisfy business needs. The reality today is that:

- **Information and IT are pervasive.** Everything can and is being digitized in some way.
- **IT literacy is increasing.** People enter the workforce expecting the same level of connectivity and user-friendly tools they have at home.
- **Demand for IT solutions continues to exceed supply.** It is frustrating to have a need stuck in IT backlog with the knowledge that it may take months or even years to deliver valuable functionality.
- **Cloud services are proliferating.** There is a growing range of low entry cost and effective solutions available for almost every apparent business need—such as Software as a Service (SaaS), and Infrastructure as a Service (IaaS).

As a result of these forces, the high priests and priestesses of IT are no longer the only source of IT talent. In some ways, that cat was out of the proverbial bag with the invention of the mini-computer and given free reign with the invention of the PC and spreadsheet tools like VisiCalc. These tools enabled non-programmers to quickly do the work of a highly-skilled programmer, usually in a fraction of the time.

> *The high priests and priestesses of IT are no longer the only source of IT talent*

Shadow IT

The risk of sharing the IT technology domain with the business is often referred to as *shadow IT*. In most organizations, shadow IT is considered a scourge on the landscape that must be eliminated. Sometimes called *stealth IT*, shadow IT usually means work that should be performed within the formal IT organization, but is performed instead by non-IT professionals inside business units.

The impact of shadow IT can include systems that don't meet requirements of security, privacy, integrity, or compliance with standards such as Sarbanes-Oxley/SOX, GDPR, Basel II or PCI DSS. The degree to which shadow IT solutions violate such standards, and the implications of such violations, is rarely considered.

The problem with painting IT work handled outside the IT organization with the shadow IT brush is that it misses a key trend and, ultimately, a powerful opportunity for Business-IT convergence.

The Cause of Shadow IT

Shadow IT groups are often symptoms of unmet (or poorly met) demand. As such, they are prevalent in low Business-IT Maturity environments where demand appetite exceeds supply capability so demand creates its own supply. Paradoxically, they are also prevalent in very high Business-IT Maturity environments—although in this context they would probably never be referred to as shadow IT. More likely they would be classified as *power users* of embedded IT capabilities that are encouraged and celebrated as indicators of high maturity.

It is important to understand why shadow IT exists. If it is generated by low IT maturity, shadow IT needs to be integrated into the formal, sanctioned, budgeted IT

From Feeding Them to Teaching Them to Fish

In 2007, I predicted that in the future there will be new and different roles to play for the IT professional with the emphasis on DIFFERENT. Today's IT organization has to carefully rethink the range of IT capabilities needed by the enterprise it serves, and how best to meet those capabilities—and not just from within the IT organization.

IT professionals have to consider an entire ecosystem including the business users as producers, external entities as producers and consumers, and new internal roles of brokers, guides, and information assistants.

I don't know exactly what all the roles will be, what they will be called, where they will work, what competencies they will need, or how they will be sourced and trained. But I do believe they will not be configured in anything like today's typical IT organization where dozens, or hundreds, or in some cases thousands of IT professionals are doing IT stuff for the business.

As IT professionals, we must shift our emphasis from fishing for the masses, to teaching them to fish, at the same time providing them with fishing rods, well stocked lakes to fish in, and guidance as to where and how to fish.

Shadow IT: The Good, The Bad, and the Ugly

Shadow IT is a big issue in the context of teaching the business to fish. It's one that needs more air in the context of IT transformation. Shadow IT is nearly always cast as a negative phenomenon and something to be avoided, challenged, even eliminated.

As an example, Information Week published an article entitled "Shadow IT: 8 Ways to Cope" (March 18, 2015). While all the suggested coping mechanisms make sense, I'm always concerned that shadow IT is treated as an evil force to be eradicated as opposed to a powerful capability to be encouraged and leveraged in ways that make business sense.

I am reminded of shadow IT whenever I work with a client with a neglected IT capability. Often a new CIO has been brought in (the first sign that a previously neglected IT capability is now getting some attention) and he asks me to help him review the global IT operating model. Among the challenges this CIO faces are a number of Shadow IT groups: small groups of people doing IT work in the company, but outside of officially sanctioned IT organization, budget, governance, accountability or responsibilities.

Conversely, whenever I come across known/recognized shadow IT groups, I always wonder about other unknown shadow IT groups that might be lurking so deep in the corners that they are virtually invisible.

operating model. If, on the other hand, shadow IT is a result of high maturity, then the right infrastructure needs to be provided to support it, and it should be prodded and encouraged.

There is a reason that shadow IT should be eliminated in low maturity environments. First and foremost, because shadow IT is a symptom of low maturity. To eliminate it, the organization has to commit to (and act upon) improving the state of IT capabilities. This is a good thing. Additionally shadow IT groups are often unwitting impediments to improving IT capability. For example:

- If a CIO doesn't have control over the entire IT budget, then IT spend is sub-optimized.
- If a CIO doesn't have control over IT standards, processes, and practices, then improving IT capability is that much more difficult .The point here is not whether IT capabilities should be embedded in the business or not. They absolutely should. But exactly what to embed, when to embed it, and how to embed it are important questions that must be thought about as part of the IT operating model design.

Bringing Shadow IT into the Light

The real danger of shadow IT is when it is truly hidden in the shadows, when the real costs of IT are buried, when the risks associated with legal or regulatory compliance is real, or when solutions have high risk or low integrity.

The best way to head off this danger is to go with the flow inherent in Business-IT convergence, and to encourage embedded IT by providing the infrastructure to bring shadow IT into the light where it can be safely guided and supported. There is valuable information to be discovered by shining the light on shadow IT. For example:

1. What needs does shadow IT fulfill, and why aren't those needs fulfilled by official IT groups?
2. How are shadow IT groups and activities staffed and funded, and how can these activities be legitimized and leveraged?
3. How can an infrastructure be established that includes appropriate governance and funding mechanisms for shadow IT that clearly delineate departmental needs and solutions from those that should be leveraged across departments or the entire enterprise?
4. What is the best way to connect Business Relationship Managers with embedded IT groups?
5. What is the nature of the role within other groups that may be filling a business relationship management role? Can these roles be transitioned into a more standardized, consistent BRM capability?

There is other valuable knowledge embedded within shadow IT groups. For example:

1. What types of knowledge exist in shadow IT groups?
2. Are there ways to capture and tap into this knowledge?
3. Are there other groups that don't have access to this knowledge that could benefit from it?
4. What other knowledge could these groups benefit from?
5. What is the best way to make the missing knowledge available to those that need it?

The lesson here is if you can't beat shadow IT, embrace it! By looking at shadow IT as a positive rather than a negative force—as a source of information and knowledge, and as an early form of Business-IT convergence—it is possible to bring it out of the shadows and help establish it as a part of a highly effective, enterprise-wide IT operating model.

> *If you can't beat shadow IT, embrace it!*

Tackling Shadow IT With Tough Love

There is a tough love aspect to tackling shadow IT groups. When I was a kid growing up in London, UK, I went to a school where uniforms were de rigueur, complete with school caps. I was caught once too often without wearing my school cap and was sent to the Vice Headmaster's office for a dressing down.

Fortunately for me, the Vice Headmaster was a wonderful man with a sense of humor, a Royal Air force mustache and manner, and a vintage Rolls-Royce to boot. He gave me one of life's great lessons: that it was not about wearing a school cap, per se. It was actually about setting and living within defined boundaries so rebellious chaps like me could push against them without doing real harm.

Managing shadow IT is similar to a parent disciplining a child. If discipline is absent, the business will suffer from lack of controls. On the other hand, too much control can stifle performance, so balance is required.

When the CIO (with appropriate support of the CEO and executive team) announces that all IT will be managed under a single IT budget, and that all IT-related resources report to the CIO's organization, this sends a message to the firm: We are raising the bar on IT. People may not like it, but they will like the fact that someone is getting serious about improving the performance of the IT function.

Often the prediction that this will create a real stink and lots of resistance, is far from what actually happens. Instead, people are likely to say: "About time. Please take this group back into IT. It is where they belong and where they will have the best growth and career opportunities."

So if shadow IT is a problem, don't hesitate. Tackle it head on as an integral part of the IT transformation plan with tough love. Be ready for the noise and resistance, but don't let that derail the transformation initiative.

The Digital Enterprise IT Capability

Carolyn Marvin, in her book *When Old Technologies Were New* (1988), describes the early days of electrification when most large companies had a vice president of electrification. That role has now disappeared.

In the same way, the time may come when the chief information officer (CIO) role becomes a relic of a bygone era. Although the CIO role has not yet disappeared, it has changed significantly in the last few decades. Many CIOs today have expanded their scope to include a range of enterprise shared services. Some have responsibility for at least one major business process (e.g., supply chain). Others have morphed into *chief innovation officers*.

That raises a question. If information is everywhere and IT is ubiquitous, is there a role for chief information officers? Does the role get closer to (or merge with) the chief finance officer role (CFO) and assume the fiduciary and legal responsibilities that come with it? Or does the role disappear in the same way that the chief electrification officer did when competing electric supply systems (AC, DC), and huge centralized motors evolved into electricity as a common utility available to the masses with tiny motors distributed to the point of application?

To answer this question, it may help to think in terms of two different types of IT:

- **Infrastructure:** the common and shared base of IT capability and services used across the enterprise
- **Applications:** those things that sit on top of infrastructure but are specialized to address a specific business needs

Simply stated, there must be a single point of coordination for IT infrastructure, but not necessarily for business-specific applications which, one could argue, should be organizationally located within the business function or business process that needs them.

> *There must be a single point of coordination for IT infrastructure, but not necessarily for business-specific applications*

The problem with this line of reasoning is that things shift over time. What was yesterday's business-specific application may well be today's IT infrastructure. In fact, what was proprietary IT infrastructure today may well migrate to public, open infrastructure tomorrow. The tendency for capabilities to drift either way across the demand-supply interface complicates the challenge of managing an effective Business-IT engagement model.

Managing this trend over time calls for a continuous examination of IT services and capabilities, and decision making about what should be common and standardized versus what should be allowed to evolve with changing business needs.

Another way of splitting the IT world is into IT demand management and supply management roles. This model is becoming increasingly common, with IT leaders (sometimes called CIO or CTO) centrally coordinating the supply side of IT and business units or, increasingly, business process-focused mini-CIOs leading the demand side.

IT Organizational Clarity

The concept of Organizational Clarity is clearly laid out in Patrick Lencioni's leadership fable, *The Four Obsessions of an Extraordinary Executive: A Leadership Fable (2000).* Organizational clarity is particularly important for IT leaders today as IT management and operational roles are increasingly dispersing throughout the business rather than being performed within a homogeneous IT organization.

> *A signal that IT transformation is needed is a lack of organization clarity*

A signal that IT transformation is needed is a lack of organization clarity. The organization either will not be effective or will never know how effective it is if stakeholders are unsure about who does what when, how they do it, why they do it, how they know it was done well, and who owns the major outcomes.

Common Symptoms Reveal Lack of Organizational Clarity

Organizational clarity is like boat racing in the Olympics. The sight of eight rowers accompanied by a coxswain steering and shouting commands to help the crew keep the cadence and stroke is a compelling image. There is enormous power in the boat when all the rowers are in perfect harmony and staying on course. If the coxswain makes a mistake, or if any of the rowers fail to follow the guidance, havoc reigns. The boat slows down, or goes off course.

IT organizations that lack organizational clarity are like the slow boat in the race or, even worse, the fast boat heading in the wrong direction. The symptoms described below are just that—symptoms. They are not root causes of lack of organizational clarity.

Lack of Clear Communication

IT leadership often admits that *we don't communicate well*. Not only has virtually every IT organization raised this complaint, few, if any, IT organizations claim they communicate really well.

This is a non-trivial symptom of lack of organizational clarity. Inability to communicate clearly leads to redundant work, leakage of business value (i.e., value that should have been captured, could have been captured, but is not captured), and a general sense of confusion and disorientation.

For the beneficiaries of IT work, lack of communication clarity contributes to a poor customer experience. Customers can be heard to complain: *In IT the left hand doesn't know what the right hand is doing* or *IT doesn't have clear accountability*. The communications issue cannot be solved by mandating—or even organizing for—better communications.

IT leaders frequently talk about putting a marketing/communications specialist on their staff to address the communications problems. Improved marketing skills and disciplines for IT leadership teams is a often a good idea. But adding a communications role without addressing underlying dysfunctions and misalignments rarely, if ever, resolves communication issues.

Communications problems are symptomatic of a lack of organizational clarity

Communications problems are symptomatic of a lack of organizational clarity, not just for the IT organization as a whole, but for its moving parts such as IT infrastructure, enterprise architecture, and solutions delivery.

Lack of Clear Accountability

Another symptom of lack of organization clarity is failure to be clear about who is accountable for what and, more to the point, what happens when something goes wrong.

This is often (and unfortunately) referred to as *not knowing whose throat to choke*, but is probably more constructively thought of as *not knowing what actions to take to ensure that this error is not repeated*.

This symptom means that managers and individual performers often do not understand how their work contributes to the overall mission and vision of the enterprise and, more importantly, how it contributes to the success of internal and external customers.

Accountability issues cannot be addressed simply by mandating accountability. Unless an IT capability has clear goals, service definition, and guiding principles along with appropriate processes, roles, competencies, tools, and technologies, mandating accountability will accomplish very little except frustration among diligent members of the organization.

Lack of Role Clarity

Internal IT organizations often like to say *we run IT like a business*. Upon closer examination, however, it is clear to see that they rarely do. If they did, they would ensure role and operating model clarity to maintain a thriving business.

Role confusion is an insidious issue. Lack of role clarity leads to errors, miscommunication, redundancy, noise, and wasted effort. It creates frustration, confusion and, for a provider such as an IT organization, it leads to poor customer experience, and to the familiar refrain that IT costs too much, delivers too little, and is hard to do business with.

> *Order-taker mentality creates misunderstandings and is often seen as more of a barrier to real improvement than as an enabler*

Another complaint is that IT wants to help the business improve processes at the same time that IT processes are badly broken.

The typical IT mantra *IT exists to support the business* leads to an order-taker mentality within IT organizations. Typically, these organizations are extremely busy (to the point of rampant overwork), and yet are seen by the business as adding little value. Order-taker mentality creates misunderstandings, and is often seen as more of a barrier to real improvement than as an enabler.

It is interesting to note that external providers generally don't have a problem with role clarity. They demonstrate high maturity and a level of precision in how processes, roles, and rules of engagement are defined. In order to survive, they have to.

Role clarity is crucial to how external providers, consultants, and contractors make money, and how they attract and retain clients and talent. Their search for role clarity ends with the development of strategic and operating model clarity.

Link Between Organizational Clarity and Capability Maturity

The ultimate gauge of IT organizational clarity is in the health of the IT organization, and the business results to which it contributes. However, there are all sorts of demand-side complexities in assessing these outcomes. And, in this discussion, the notion of capability maturity is a worthy proxy for, and predictor of, end results and the ability to continuously improve.

Improving organizational clarity and, in turn increasing focus, effectiveness, and maturity, must be tackled in two dimensions:
1. **Bounding IT scope appropriately** by defining the unit of analysis. An appropri-

ate unit of analysis is commonly referred to as an IT capability. Typical IT organizations can be described by seven to nine capabilities such as IT infrastructure, enterprise architecture, opportunity discovery, solution delivery and portfolio management.

2. **Defining IT capability characteristics,** including purpose, commitment, ability, and accountability.

Defining IT Capability

The distinction between IT capabilities and IT processes is important. However, before IT capability can be clearly defined, terminology must be clarified: service, process, and capability. Refer to *Governance & Convergence, Value Chain, and Enabling Capabilities* (p. 44) and *An Approach to Operating Model Design* (p. 49).

Service

A service, in the context of IT capabilities, is best described as the interface point between a provider and a consumer where value is exchanged. Services should be defined from the perspective of the consumer. They need to be discoverable, and the service interface must be understood by the consumer. Consumers need to have clarity on what specific services do, what they cost, how they are invoked, and how problems are reported and resolved.

The service provider should have a good understanding of the value received by the consumer as well as the overall quality of the customer experience. This may comprise both tangible and intangible elements—most of which are ultimately subjective.

Debating IT Capabilities and Processes

Debates on the difference between capabilities and processes often proceed along the following lines:

> We have assessed that your (fill in the blank) capability is low, not in place or only partially in place.

Which generates the client response:

> That's wrong. We have processes and artifacts to do (fill in the blank). They are fully in place, or at least mostly in place.

To which we respond:

> The people with the role to deliver the capability associated with that process either don't know about it or are ignoring it. The result is that you don't have the capability maturity you need to (fill in the blank).

Process

A process is a sequence of interdependent and linked procedures which, at every stage, consume one or more resources (employee time, energy, money) to convert inputs (data, material, etc.) into outputs. These outputs often serve as inputs for the next stage until a known goal or outcome is reached.

Processes describe what work should be done, where inputs come from and outputs go to, what results should look like, how results should be measured and evaluated, how efficient and effective the process is, and how the process should be evaluated and improved.

Processes are driving (or at least, shaping) behavior when:
1. A process definition is known by, and used by, impacted stakeholders.
2. The process is defined at a level appropriate to its purpose.
3. The process provides best practice examples of input criteria, exit criteria, and deliverables for each major step.
4. The process clearly spells out all roles associated with each step.
5. Roles call out or point to descriptions of competencies (knowledge, skills, and behaviors) needed to satisfy a given role.
6. Outcome and in-process metrics are defined, and are used to drive continuous improvement.
7. Once familiarized with the formal process, a new person can step into the work mid-flight, and would know what to expect (and where to find) the work that has been done so far, and the steps to be performed next.
8. Defined approaches (e.g., risk management) ensure that key process steps have been followed.

Capability

Capabilities bring in the dimensions of people and technologies that use processes to get work done. Some capabilities (typically those whose primary value proposition is operational excellence) require rigorous and robust process definitions, for example frameworks such as ITIL and COBIT. Other capabilities, where the value proposition is customer intimacy or innovation, have a far higher human content requiring special competencies and judgment. In these cases processes may be less rigorously defined, but they are still important—even if only in the form

> *Capabilities, where the value proposition is customer intimacy or innovation, have a far higher human content requiring special competencies and judgment*

Reflecting on Major IT Capabilities
- *Which capabilities are supported by good processes?*
- *Where are the biggest gaps?*
- *What would be gained if the gaps were closed?*
- *Would closing the gaps help with communications both internal to the organization and with business partners?*
- *Would it help clarify roles, responsibilities and accountabilities?*
- *Would it help clarify the rules of engagement?*
- *Would it make work more predictable and more easily repeatable?*
- *Would it help identify non-value adding steps and activities, or missing roles?*
- *Would it enable process improvement and innovation initiatives?*
- *Would it help bring new employees or partners up to speed more quickly—i.e., would it accelerate time to value?*
- *What would that all be worth?*
- *What is standing in the way?*

of a checklist for the major steps, entry and exit criteria, and examples of the deliverables they create or outcomes which they are intended to produce.

A capability can be thought of as everything it takes behind the scenes to make a service possible. This will include:
- One or more processes
- Descriptions of roles needed to perform one or more procedures within a process (e.g., project manager, business analyst, relationship manager)
- Descriptions of the competencies needed to perform a given role, what the person performing the role needs to know (e.g., business knowledge), what skills they need (e.g., facilitation), and what behaviors they should exhibit (e.g., results orientation)
- An adequate supply of competent human resources filling the defined roles
- Tools and technologies needed to automate or execute necessary processes or procedures
- Management systems necessary to ensure the health and performance of the capability—including funding, organizational will, and personal incentives

Three Classes of IT Capabilities
IT capabilities fall into one of three different classes as shown in the graphic on page 44:
1. Value chain capabilities

2. Alignment and governance capabilities
3. Enabling capabilities

Value Chain Capabilities

At the core of the value chain are capabilities that take inputs, add value, and deliver outputs to customers or end consumers. In the world of IT, these outputs tend to be services and products.

It may be useful to think of value chain capabilities as those that the end customer appreciates (hopefully), and is willing to pay money for.

For example, business users may have a business problem they would like IT to help solve. That problem (or opportunity) is the input to a value chain. The first capability that will address that problem adds value by analyzing the problem, and identifying and proposing a solution. Business users appreciate that value has been added—drill-

---

Not All IT Capabilities Are Equal

The distinctions between Value Chain, Enabling, and Governance and Convergence Capabilities are significant for the following reasons:

- **Different types of IT capabilities tend to be optimized towards different value propositions**, *with implications for how they are organized. For example, enabling capabilities tend to be optimized for operational excellence (as shared services, they need to deliver predictable, consistent, quality services at the lowest possible cost). Value chain capabilities tend to be organized for customer intimacy, delivering what specific customers want; anticipating customer needs.*

- **Alignment and governance capabilities tend to be more about decision-making than delivering services.** *They make decisions or provide decision-making frameworks. Think enterprise architecture and the mechanisms and structures that support it as alignment and governance mechanisms. These tend to be networked to link stakeholders and decision makers and optimized to maximize the business value delivered or enabled by IT Investments.*

- **Some types of IT capabilities lend themselves to alternate sourcing more than others.** *For example, aligning and governance capabilities lend themselves the least to outsourcing (do you want to pass decision rights to an external vendor?)*

- **Different types of IT capabilities lend themselves to different funding models.** *For example, value chain capabilities lend themselves to direct business funding, whereas enabling capabilities lend themselves better to indirect funding models (e.g., overhead charge).*

---

ing into their stated problem, and offering (and perhaps demonstrating via a proto-type) one or more proposed solutions.

The next capability in the value chain might take the chosen solution, and develop and deploy that solution. From the perspective of the business user, value has been clearly added by taking a proposed solution and delivering it. The final capability that adds value is supporting and maintaining that solution. Again, this is another recognizable way of adding value for the customer. Ultimately, the only capabilities that business users or consumers care about and are willing to pay for (directly or indirectly) are those that

> *The only capabilities that business users or consumers care about and are willing to pay for are those that provide value to them*

provide value to them. Unfortunately, while these value chain capabilities are necessary, they are not sufficient by themselves.

Governance and Convergence Capabilities

Value chain capabilities typically depend upon other enabling capabilities that ensure that the work they are doing is aligned and governed in a way that ensures the capabilities are operating effectively and in the interests of the enterprise.

For example, determining which business problems will be addressed, which solutions will be selected, and how staff and resources will be allocated, are all important controls that value chain capabilities will be subject to.

Governance and convergence capabilities govern what enters the value chain, expectations for value to be added by the value chain, harvesting of expected business value and decision rights, and accountabilities associated with the enterprise.

Enabling Capabilities

Value chain capabilities and governance and convergence capabilities typically draw upon other capabilities that enable them. Enabling capabilities can be thought of as shared services that are common to other capabilities or to other instances of problems/solutions working their way through the value chain.

Examples of IT services that might enable the value chain capabilities include:
- Project management
- IT operations
- IT supply

Optimal Number of IT Capabilities

The optimal number of IT capabilities used in a capability model depends on the mission to be served by a given capability. But more importantly, it is a question of granularity. Picking the right granularity for an end-to-end process is crucial and perhaps as much art as science. It has more to do with the characteristics of and limitations to the workings of the human mind than anything else.

Three IT capabilities is probably too little granularity to be useful in terms of analytical and management discipline. On the other hand, twelve or more IT capabilities is probably too much granularity. Experience shows that between seven and nine is the right number of IT capabilities to have in a top-level IT capability model. You know you are at the right level of decomposition when to go one level deeper would insult the intelligence of the people who perform the process.

Optimal Level of Capability Decomposition

When modeling IT capabilities, a single capability can only be understood in reference to the level of detailed process below it. At least two levels of decomposition are necessary. Beyond that, the optimal level of capabilities in the model depends on the number required to understand or improve the capability,

Consider for example, the process aspect of an IT capability. Capabilities that are highly procedural, such as those found in IT infrastructure and operations, typically need more levels of decomposition. (Coincidentally, this is the domain of ITIL, so process definitions and a process architecture can be purchased off-the-shelf.)

On the other hand, a capability such as opportunity discovery may be more about analytical skills and the magical space between problem understanding and solution identification. This space is much more about people with specialized skills and specific business domain knowledge than about sequential, detailed and rigorously controlled processes (such as statistical process control).

Assessing the Effectiveness of IT Capabilities

One clue to the need for IT transformation is the suitability and health of IT capabilities, including the processes upon which those capabilities depend. An IT capability assessment typically examines two different kinds of capabilities. Frequently the second set of IT capabilities is of greater significance than the first:

1. IT capabilities that are largely owned and executed by the IT organization. For example, capabilities and processes needed to:
   - Manage the IT infrastructure

- • Deliver business solutions
- • Manage the IT organization
2. IT capabilities that are jointly owned by business and IT, such as capabilities and processes required to:
   - • Manage the Business-IT portfolio
   - • Manage Business-IT relationships
   - • Manage enterprise architecture

IT Improvement vs. Innovation

A key issue in planning an IT transformation is the degree to which an incremental, or radical, approach to change is called for. The issues here relate to speed, depth, and breadth of change.

In his book, *Managerial Breakthrough (1964)*, Joseph Juran distinguished between continuous and breakthrough improvement (i.e., innovation). Continuous improvement (TQM, Six sigma, etc.) is about improving the performance of a process (or product). This is a mostly incremental approach.

Innovation (what Juran referred to as breakthrough) is a much more radical approach. Today, innovation is often called re-engineering. Innovation is, by definition, not incremental, and performance gains can be orders of magnitude. The competencies, management styles, methods, and organizational approaches to improvement versus innovation are quite different.

Juran proposed a cycle of improvement and breakthrough (shown in the left-hand chart below). The cycle improves things until the marginal effort is no longer justified by the

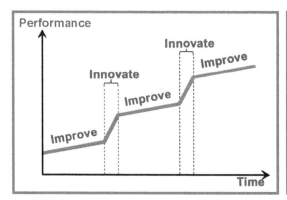

Juran Improve-Innovate Cycle   *Improve-Innovate Matrix for Products & Processes*

marginal performance gain, or until a new technology or method promises significant gains from a new way of doing things.

Once the innovation (innovated product or re-engineered process) has been introduced, the cycle shifts back to continuous improvement by applying methods to stabilize, and incrementally improve, the new product or process.

> *Once innovation has been introduced, the cycle shifts back to continuous improvement*

This improve-innovate cycle can be applied to products (or services) and processes. IT organizations need to develop strong competencies in all four quadrants of the figure (shown in the right-hand chart on the previous page), as these apply to both IT processes and products (or services), and to business processes and products (or services).

Continuous Quality Improvement Management

As the IT industry moves from Web 1.0 to Web 2.0, from ERP to software as a service (SaaS), from process improvement and integration to collaboration, process and product innovation, methods (such as ITIL and CMMI) are table stakes for playing in the business innovation space with significantly higher business value.

The journey from Business-IT Maturity Level 1 to Maturity Level 2 (described in Chapter 2) is largely about control and continuous improvement and putting controls in place for predictable, stable, and reliable services. The journey from Level 2 to Level 3 is largely about breakthrough. It can't be reached with a control mindset.

Remembering that this is all about the maturity model introduced in Chapter 2. The real challenge is that the Level 1 and low-Level 2 requirements never go away. It is important to keep all the good process and quality improvement work that moved the organization to Level 2 at the same time shifting focus from the IT supply side to the business demand side. This transitional step is when breakthrough disciplines can be applied.

As a broad generalization and over-simplification, continuous quality improvement management (control) on the supply capabilities must be mastered to mature beyond Level 1, then innovation management (breakthrough) must be mastered to move to Level 3.

While change doesn't always begin at the top (though it often does), transformational change is ultimately led from the top. Some CIOs are much better at leading control-oriented IT organizations. Other CIOs are better at leading organizations that are breakthrough-oriented.

Few CIOs are equally adept at leading both and, therefore, capable of leading their IT organizations on the entire journey from Level 1 to Level 3. IT leadership is about more than the CIO. The CIO's leadership team, IT managers and, ultimately, everyone in the IT organization has a leadership role.

However, when CIOs do not bring the right leadership style and focus to organizational transformation (e.g., breakthrough to get from Level 2 to Level 3), their leadership teams are unlikely to do so. If the IT leadership team is not bringing the right style and focus, it is highly unlikely that IT managers will.

Towards Collaborative, Emergent Change

While the distinctions between continuous improvement and innovation discussed earlier are important at lower Levels of Business-IT maturity, reaching Level 3 demands a more organically-based approach to change.

Reaching Level 3 demands a more organically-based approach to change

At higher maturity, the mechanistic trappings of organization charts and narrow job descriptions must give way to more flexible organizational thinking. Here, clues from the science of chaos and complexity present a more-realistic context for transformation. Rigid organization structures must give way to a more agile *plug and play* approach to organizational design.

Change *pushed* from the top down must be replaced with a more-collaborative *pull* from those closest to doing the work—the ones who must change their knowledge, skills, and behaviors. This topic is covered in more detail in Chapter 8.

Organization Transformation and Operating Model Design

Perhaps in the days of hierarchical, authoritarian organizations or in the early days of the industrial revolution a determinist approach to operating model design was feasible. That assumption holds only if the organization could be frozen in some future, transformed state after all transformational activities are complete.

The fallacy is this: although change agents, organization leadership, and some staff members may know the characteristics they would like to see in the future state, and the kinds of behaviors they would like to experience, how to get to that future state, and the design of the new operating model is far less certain. Operating model design today is about emergence that occurs when leadership points people in the right direction then gets out of their way.

To facilitate that emergence, the first objective is to define the *right direction* including:
1. Desired outcomes
2. Capabilities to be achieved by those outcomes

Chaos, Complexity and the Future of the IT Organization

In Chapter 3, I alluded to the climb from Level 1 to Level 2 Business-IT Maturity as bringing order to the chaos, while the Level 2 to Level 3 journey is about managing complexity, decentralizing control with safe boundaries and empowering the community of IT stakeholders.

Although this is a difficult concept for many people to get their heads around, it is a concept that can be especially informative for IT professionals whose lives depend upon driving out ambiguity, bringing order to chaos, and bringing processes under control.

In 1992, I read Margaret Wheatley's remarkable book, Leadership and the New Science (1992). Wheatley's book gave me a new lens through which to see the world of organizational change and a new set of tools and approaches for working with my clients. It was intriguing to me at the time though hard to translate into action. I followed up my reading of this book by participating in a multi-day workshop led by Meg Wheatley in Toronto. The experience was personally transformational.

At that time I was leading research into both IT effectiveness and organizational change and transformation, and I knew that much of the conventional wisdom about organizations and transformation did not seem to apply or was, at best, of limited value. While working with a large State agency, I persuaded the visionary CIO to let me try some of the techniques I had learned in an IT leadership workshop.

We allowed people to drown in an apparently overwhelming sea of data. This helped them clarify the current situation and allowed a new, natural order to emerge. At the same time, executives began to trust the ability of people to find new order in chaos and to simplify their work environment.

Although this approach was a little scary at times, the results were spectacular and my fear of taking a client through an unpredictable process disappeared.

3. Processes, roles, competencies (i.e., knowledge, skills, and behaviors) needed to support those capabilities
4. Management and governance systems to maximize the delivery of those capabilities

The second objective involves empowering people to do what is necessary including:
1. Over-communicating items 1 through 4 listed above
2. Engaging people in understanding, co-developing, and co-creating organizational clarity
3. Enabling them with a meaningful way to participate in shaping their future

Complexity, Self-Organization, and IT

The last 15-20 years has resulted in an increase of complexity for IT leaders that creates a need to step back and rethink the nature of chaos and order and what these concepts mean for being in control.

I have experienced several types of these non-conventional interventions. I've mostly used the Wheatley approach as a workshop technique and consulting intervention. With the advent of Web 2.0 and social networking, I'm increasingly using the principles of complex adaptive systems to inform my IT organization design work.
- *They typically work with large stakeholder groups (whole systems), shun Power-Point slides, and throw out traditional artifacts such as detailed agendas.*
- *They replace hours upon hours of sitting and listening, with moving, participating, and leading.*
- *They are not only highly effective in terms of their deliverables, but they also achieve much higher buy-in and commitment for the participants than do traditional workshops, town hall meetings, and the like.*

Some of the key insights that come out of the chaos/complexity disciplines include:
- *Complex systems display non-linearity*
- *Output is not proportional to input*
- *Variety, randomness, paradox, information, and interconnection inherent in complex systems are sources of creativity*
- *Complex systems display emergent order*
- *Organization is a natural, spontaneous act*
- *Systems have a capacity to self-organize*

Ralph D. Stacey, in The Chaos Frontier (1991), captured this last insight beautifully when he defined self-organization as a process in which components of a system spontaneously communicate with each other, and cooperate in coordinated and concerted common behavior.

4. Making sure they have the right tools and infrastructure to do the job
5. Getting out of their way

A Siloed Organization Can't be Transformed Silo by Silo

Too often IT transformation initiatives surface and are managed silo by silo. This rarely works.

- **Service management is on a path to a better future**—often on a great path, but it is on its own path.
- **Enterprise architecture is on a path to a better future**—often on a great path, but it is on its own path since no one is considering the joint implications of service management and enterprise architecture.
- **Solutions delivery is on a path to a better future**—often on a great path, but it is on its own path
- **Business Relationship Management (BRM) is on a path to a better future**—often on a great path, but it is on its own path
- **Project/program/portfolio management is on a path to a better future**—often on a great path, but it is on its own path

The good news is that most of the moving parts that comprise an IT capability are moving to a better, more disciplined, and more intelligently designed future. The bad news is that:

The Trouble With IT Transformation

I've been involved in many organizational transformations, some globally, over 40 years of management consulting. Most were with IT organizations. Many were with HR organizations. Some were transformations to global shared services (typically embracing IT, HR, finance and facilities.) My takeaways include the following:

- *"You aren't any good and you have to transform" can feel demeaning and is a bitter pill to swallow. And is almost always untrue, at least in part. Attacking a team is not the best way to enroll people in change.*
- *Organizational transformation is painful and ultimately fails to deliver on its promises. Announcing yet another transformation initiative typically elicits a "Here we go again" response.*
- *Organizational transformations tend to promise too much and deliver too little.*
- *The current state transformation to future state model no longer applies. Transformation implies a journey from current state to a future state by going through some kind of radical change.*
- *Transformations are highly disruptive. They assume that someone (or some group) knows what the future state looks like and that "all we have to do is to transform into that future state."*

1. They are starting from different points on a maturity curve.
2. Their destinations are usually roughly the same unless you drill down into the details (where the devil lies).
3. They are each following their own trajectories.
4. Nobody is driving this holistically. It is a set of relatively independent transformations.

Before each of the silos began transforming, work got done through a combination of:
- **Tribal knowledge** characterized by comments like: *I know who to go to because the go-to person has worked here for years*.
- **Heroic efforts.** Processes are either broken or undefined but that is fine because *someone can always be found who will fix things and be the hero*, and heroic behavior is rewarded.

Before the transformation, things muddled along. They were error prone, inefficient, and frustrating to the business customer, but they worked. Now in the heat of transformation people:
- Position for power and influence
- Protect turf
- Are unable to see (or believe) the big picture of the end state
- Are afraid of losing control (reflected in comments like: "The old ways were not very efficient, but at least we understood them.")
- Remain so focused on their own silo they don't have time, energy, or structural paths to clarify how all the moving parts engage

The Changing State of Organizational Change
Increasingly, organizations that are healthy, effective, and growing in capability are in a state of constant change and adoption. In most situations, they don't need to be forced into an artificial state of change.

The reality is that organizational behavior is too complex for anyone to know what the future state will look like.

The Only Constant is Change
Even though we cannot predict the future of IT with certainty, we can and must accept that the constant IS change and will never become a fixed status quo. Just as all living organisms evolve, so do organizations. The question is, are we heading the right direction given the dynamic forces that impact our future? Is our evolution purposeful, or are we simply at the mercy of the prevailing winds?

Business Relationship Management: Catalyst for a Digital Revolution

5

Trust is a crucial element of strategic partnerships—
difficult to earn, easy to lose, and almost impossible to regain once lost

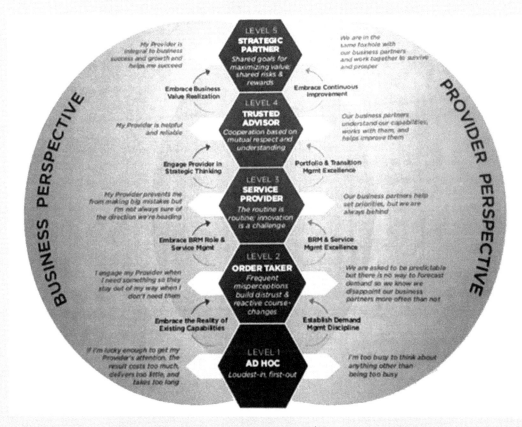

Business Relationship Maturity Model, BRM Body of Knowledge (BRMBOK™), Business Relationship Management Institute, Inc., Copyright and all rights reserved. Material from this publication has been reproduced with the permission of BRM Institute

BRMs stimulate, surface and shape business demand for IT projects, services, capabilities and investments in order to maximize their business value

Overview

This Chapter examines the foundations of Business Relationship Management (BRM), one of the key IT management innovations since the first data processing departments surfaced in the 1960s. It reviews the context for BRM and how this innovation came about. It also examines how the BRM role is evolving and discusses some of the thornier issues such as reporting lines, accountabilities, and job titles.

Business Relationship Management: Catalyst for a Digital Revolution

Defining the Business Relationship Management Role

Business Relationship Management has been gaining popularity as a key position that sits between a provider (most frequently IT) and its business partners. Rarely titled Business Relationship Manager, this role represents IT to the business and the business to IT. This is an internal role that should not be confused with the similarly titled externally-facing role common in banks and financial services organizations.

The IT Service Management movement placed BRM in its standards as a tactical process, largely focused on steady-state IT services. Providing high quality, steady-state services is certainly an important aspect for any IT organization, but once business partners experience BRM in a purely tactical role as negotiator for, and arbiter of, services and service levels, they are unlikely to invite BRM to the next strategy offsite to help define how business strategy can leverage digitization.

The Typical BRM

The most common BRM model includes these functions:

- **Stimulates, surfaces, and shapes business demand** for IT projects, services, capabilities, and investments in order to maximize their business value. This means taking a proactive role in educating business partners, suppressing demand for low value activities, while stimulating demand for high value activities.
- **Contributes to business strategy and planning** as a member of both business and IT leadership teams
- **Identifies how information and IT can support and advance business objectives,** and helps translate demand into supply
- **Helps create project and program charters**
- **Oversees initiatives and helps manage business process change** to ensure that

Context for Business Relationship Management

BRM has figured prominently in my career since the early 1990s. At that time I was a new partner with Ernst & Young (E&Y) in their Center for Business Innovation leading a multi-company research program that evolved into a 3-year longitudinal study of IT leadership and transformation. The Aha! moment for me came from a side conversation at one of the research meetings with the global CIO of a large corporation. He was taking his company on an IT transformation journey, a key part of which was outsourcing, leaving a small retained staff. He wanted to know more about the role of partner at E&Y.

I recall him saying, "I can call my E&Y partner at 5 PM on a Friday with a business problem and he will have a team of the right people in our offices on Monday morning, fully equipped with the tools and technologies they need to hit the ground running. I don't know how you do that. I don't know how you hire the right talent, develop that talent, recognize and reward that talent. I don't know how you fund business development and practice management and other non-billable hours. I'd like to know."

He went on to explain that his vision was for the majority of retained staff to be roughly the equivalent of E&Y partners and he needed to better understand that role. This role became known as Business Relationship Management. I was subsequently engaged by that CIO to work with three leading academics to develop a Relationship Management competency model and training program and to deliver the initial courses. We delivered the first course in early 1996.

Fast forward to 2005. I was on the faculty of The Concours Institute working with Professor James Cash (Harvard Business School), my colleague Dr. Keri Pearlson, now Executive Director of the Cybersecurity Research Consortium at the MIT Sloan School, and other luminaries. In 2007 we launched a Relationship Management Leadership Development Program. Once again I was tapped to develop and teach part of this course and to coach participants through the training.

Fast forward again, this time to 2011, when a quintuple heart bypass operation put me on the sidelines for a while. With time on my hands, I hung out at home perusing the web. I joined a small LinkedIn group called Professional Business Relationship Managers that I found to be a very active and interesting group. After a while Aaron Barnes, the group's moderator, invited me to co-moderate the group. Meanwhile the group was growing quickly so we decided to invite a third moderator: Dr. Aleksandr Zhuk who had become an active and insightful group member.

In January 2013, the three of us discussed our plans for the LinkedIn group. At the end of what was the most exciting telephone call in my professional life, we agreed to start a Business Relationship Management Institute as a non-profit organization. It has been an incredible joy for me to see how a global BRM community has come together and support each other on their journeys in pursuit of business value and Business-IT convergence.

the value predicted by a business case is actually realized

- **Monitors business partner customer experience**, and facilitates continuous improvement in that experience

If that sounds like a lot of responsibility, it is. At their best, IT BRMs are thought of as mini-CIOs leveraging shared IT infrastructure, common applications, and enterprise systems, while overseeing business unit-specific IT needs. BRMs who are successful in this role are often on a succession path to the CIO position. In fact, the CIO is in many ways the über-relationship manager, setting the tone for demand shaping and the strategic context for IT, and typically owning the Business-IT relationships with the most senior executive team. Competencies required of the BRM role include:

Driving Value Realization
Driving value realization might be the most important competency for a BRM. It includes knowing how to surface, clarify, and promote the best value-delivering opportunities for IT investments and assets, and how to ensure that these actually deliver on their promised value—delivered in ways that are felt and seen. This requires skills in program and project management, portfolio management, influence and persuasion, communication, finance, and organizational change.

Understanding the Business Environment
Driving value realization requires a deep understanding of the business, its ecosystem, and the competitive landscape. Successful BRMs have a keen sense of the top strategic business and IT issues—both short and long term—and how these issues relate to initiatives in their industry.

Driving value realization requires a deep understanding of the business, its ecosystem, and the competitive landscape

In short, they understand the *business of the business*. They are viewed by business leaders as proactive partners in finding the right solutions to business needs, not as mere order takers for IT services.

Closing Gaps Between IT and its Key Stakeholders
Business and IT leaders must be on the same page in terms of mission, vision, values, and goals for both IT and the business. Mismatches in any of these areas can damage the ability to build and sustain value-producing Business-IT relationships.

Successful BRMs work closely with business leaders to predict demand for IT services and capabilities, and to manage that demand. They are effective at managing the flow of demand through negotiations, and seek to resolve demand-supply imbalances. Most importantly, they constantly seek ways to foster Business-IT convergence by teaching business partners to fish rather than fishing for them.

Managing Relationships

Any role with the word *relationship* in the title implies a high level of competence at creating, sustaining, and developing strong, trusting relationships among stakeholders, and especially between business units and the IT groups that support them. Relationship skills do not come naturally and are not easily developed in some people. Effective BRMs are able to build and maintain relationships with senior IT and business leaders. They are seen as a value-added participant in strategic business-level discussions (i.e., worthy of a seat at the executive table).

Effective BRMs are able to build and maintain relationships with senior IT and business leaders

Facilitating Organizational Change

Facilitating organizational change requires understanding the organizational levers for effective change (people, process, and technology), and how IT and business strategies translate into practical plans of action for change. The successful change facilitator:

- **Engages in discussions with IT and business leaders** on the intended and unintended consequences of change
- **Is willing to confront senior executive sponsors** if they are not walking the talk, and proactively leading the change themselves
- **Understands the total cost**—both technical and human—of end-to-end implementation of change
- **Surfaces the hidden costs and potential obstacles** that could derail change
- **Identifies key stakeholders** at the outset of a project
- **Holds leaders accountable** for results
- **Thinks and acts in terms of business results**, not deliverables

Facilitating Projects and Programs

BRMs typically have several years of project and (ideally) program management experience. They have demonstrated competency in project management fundamentals, and in the complexities of program management. They demonstrate the ability to get things done through others, even though they may lack positional power.

Communicating Effectively

BRMs are recognized for their ability to listen, speak, write, and communicate clearly

Eight Competencies Required of individuals in the BRM Role
1. *Drive value realization*
2. *Understand the business environment*
3. *Close gaps between IT and its key stakeholders*
4. *Manage relationships*
5. *Facilitate organizational change*
6. *Facilitate projects and programs*
7. *Communicate effectively*
8. *Provide financial expertise*

and effectively. They demonstrate the ability to negotiate win-win, or at least buy-in, in situations where there are opposing viewpoints. They have the ability to recognize and surface disconnects between IT and business leaders, and are able to resolve problems.

Providing Financial Expertise
Successful BRMs have good knowledge of finance and accounting. They know their ROIs and their NPVs, and they know how to build a compelling business case. They understand portfolio management, and have at least basic knowledge of options theory. They understand the financial drivers of the business and the industry within which their company operates.

Relationship Alignment
There are at least three dimensions along which relationship managers can align with their business partners. The first two dimensions are pretty obvious, and generally handled well. The third dimension is more difficult, and is often not well addressed. These dimensions are:
1. **Domain Expertise.** Business relationship managers (by whatever title this role operates) need to really understand the business domain for which they are responsible—be it marketing, supply chain, human resources, etc. They need to have deep domain knowledge in order to bring value to their business partners and have sufficient credibility to make an impact.
2. **Geography.** As the real estate cliché goes, location, location, location. This also applies to Business Relationship Management. At its best, business relationship managers should be co-located with the senior managers of the business unit with which they are aligned. At the very least, they need easy access. The occasional fly in to meet with business partners isn't an optimal way to create and maintain

productive, trusting Business-IT partnerships.

3. **Maturity.** Skilled business relationship managers are a rare resource. The most effective and creative BRMs should be aligned with business units and executives with the highest demand maturity—i.e., with the best capacity to recognize and leverage high value IT-enabled opportunities. Innovative, change agent types of business relationship managers will quickly become frustrated facing off against executives who are technologically in the dark ages or who cherish the status quo. Similarly, progressive, innovative business leaders quickly become frustrated working with a business relationship manager who lacks drive, a sense of urgency, the creativity to generate valuable ideas about IT possibilities, and the skills to bring them to fruition.

The most effective and creative BRMs should be aligned with business units and executives with the highest demand maturity

Business Relationship Manager as Management Consultant

The partner role is traditionally offered by management consulting firms to their clients. It represents the best model for the BRM as a management consultant. The partner role in a large management consulting firm typically:

1. Owns the client (i.e., the BRMs business partner) relationship
2. Helps the client shape and clarify needs and opportunities
3. Co-creates with the client the approach to meeting needs and harnessing opportunities
4. Identifies resources to be brought to the table to address identified needs
5. Orchestrates those resources
6. Empowers the engagement team and program and/or project managers
7. Ensures that the best interests of business partners are being served at all times
8. Acts as an escalation point when necessary
9. Meets with business partners regularly to keep them informed
10. Meets with the engagement team regularly to monitor progress, understand potential barriers, and identify new opportunities

What a BRM Needs to be an Effective Management Consultant

Management consultants depend on good consulting processes, the wisdom to apply those processes with delicacy, a wide selection of management consulting tools they know how to use, and leadership who trusts them to deliver.

The greatest gifts consultants can bring to the table are the right tools and techniques, and the skills to use them. Useful tools can include:

- Frameworks to prioritize business needs and expectations based upon potential business value (e.g., Kano Model)
- Dialogic tools to surface discussion about business demand and IT supply maturity
- Stakeholder mapping tools to surface and leverage the network of actors in a planned business change
- Six-Sigma tools such as value stream mapping
- Voice of the customer and strategy tools such as scenario planning and strategy-on-a-page
- Mind mapping
- Brainstorming

Of course, having access to a toolbox does not make anyone a master consultant. Tools are valuable only when the right tool is used in the right way to provide value. An artisan who knows how to use many different types of hammers realizes that not all problems are nails.

> *Tools are valuable only when the right tool is used in the right way to provide value*

Business Relationship Maturity

The graphic on the first page of this chapter (p. 85) shows how the quality of the business partner experience grows as BRM maturity increases.

Ad Hoc Relationship

At the lowest maturity level, the BRM role has typically not been formalized. As such, it is being handled in an ad hoc way. The squeaky wheel business partner gets the most attention. Or in some cases, the least demanding business partners—regardless of their potential to use IT for high value purposes—get the most attention.

Order Taker Relationship

At this level of maturity, IT supply is often badly broken, and the Business-IT relationship is typically hostile. The BRM role is introduced to patch things up. The BRM believes the best way to improve the relationship is to say yes to any and all business demands. This approach is nearly always a losing proposition. IT can't meet the demand and, if they did, there is little to no business value to be gained.

Service Provider

At the mid-level of maturity, the importance of Service Management is recognized, often accompanied by the introduction of Service Management discipline and standards.

Putting on the Boxing Gloves

I love teaching Business Relationship Management. They say that the best way to learn is to teach, and I always learn from my course participants. I was teaching a course and went through my usual routine of asking the participants what metaphors came to mind when they think about the BRM role.

The answers are always revealing and sometimes surprising. One of the most seasoned BRMs said, "Boxer!" I was initially taken aback, but as he went on to describe his choice of metaphor, I realized what an apt metaphor boxing represents. Strong BRMs deflect low value requests. They challenge dysfunctions in the IT organization, bobbing and weaving to move the IT organization to a more responsive role. They are willing to throw a punch when necessary, appreciating that not to do so is to become a punching bag for someone who is not stepping up to the plate or is not delivering what they are supposed to deliver.

Throughout the 3-day course, the BRM who offered the boxing metaphor offered many real examples of how he had pushed back and steered his business partner away from low value requests and towards high value opportunities. He offered examples of how he had refused to collude with dysfunctional IT behavior, while stepping in to point out shortcomings in IT services or processes and offering to help fix these–once. There were no second chances. Let the business partner down a second time and you received the knockout punch.

The seasoned BRM knows how to deflect low value requests and turn them into high value opportunities, just as a boxer deflects his opponent's punches and uses his opponent's momentum to win the fight.

Trusted Advisor

This is a more constructive and productive relationship where the business partner sees the BRM as an advisor. By this time, there has usually been some formalization of the BRM role and its rules of engagement. There has also been some level of training for individuals in the BRM role, or at least some thought put into the selection of people for the role.

Strategic Partner

The holy grail of BRM implementations is to develop strategic partnerships. This should be a clear ambition, and one that is understood and shared by the BRM and business partners. It is important to recognize that partnerships aren't strategic simply because BRMs say they are or want them to be.

The elevated position of strategic partner is reached because it is earned, and because business partners perceive the BRM role that way.

IT Matures as the BRM Role Matures

At the risk of pointing out the obvious, the BRM role does not act in isolation. It is inextricably linked to IT supply. If IT supply is broken, the BRM role will be limited, and might not even mature to the level of Order Taker. This is a common situation. Things are bad, so the BRM role is introduced.

Unless supply improves, the BRM role is doomed to failure, and may actually make the situation worse when promises are made, and expectations are set that cannot be kept. On top of inadequate supply, the BRM role is seen by the business partner as overhead—more evidence that the IT team is clueless, always adding cost without demonstrating value.

> *To reach the holy grail of strategic partner, IT supply has to be excellent*

To reach the holy grail of strategic partner, IT supply has to be excellent—both with steady state services (networks, email, help desk, etc.) and with solution delivery (projects and programs). The strategic BRM needs IT supply to work flawlessly. At the same time, IT supply needs BRM to suppress low value demand while stimulating demand that delivers real business value. This creates a sustainable, virtuous cycle that makes everyone happy.

Why the Business Relationship Manager Role is Gaining Traction

There are several reasons for the increasing interest in the BRM role:

1. **IT Service Management standards** (e.g., ITIL® and ISO/IEC 20000) formalized the BRM role as a new best practice and IT service management standard. This is a mixed blessing. On the one hand it is good because it has created awareness and legitimization for the BRM role. On the other hand, it positions the BRM tactically and operationally as a champion for IT service management rather than as a strategic channel for creating business value from IT. IT service management is an important enabler of IT business value, but if that is all the BRM aspires to (or is seen as), then the value of BRM will be constrained and, sooner or later, the role will be seen as overhead.

2. **BRM as the Silver Bullet.** After years of attempts by CIOs to get their business partners to love and value the IT function, the deployment of the BRM role might be the missing bullet. At the very least, it is the next intervention to try.

3. **Emerging BRM Success.** Some BRMs are emerging naturally. Even without the

formal title or role (like Samantha in the story above), they are catching the eye of their CIO, and encouraging the introduction of a formalized BRM role.

Factors that Derail BRM Success

Among the most instructive BRM case studies are those of organizations that are on their second or third attempt to create an effective BRM role. The good news is that their leadership believes in the role sufficiently to try again after a deployment effort falls short.

The bad news is that there are many traps ready to derail BRM success. Some of these traps are created in the way that the role is defined, for example:

1. **Order-Taker.** Some novice BRMs fall into the trap of becoming order-takers. All business requests are seen as good requests, no matter what the potential to deliver real business value.
   - **The BRM role is not an order-taker.** The seasoned BRM, knows how to deflect low value requests in the same way that boxers deflect the punches of their opponents (as described on the previous page).
2. **Account Manager.** Some novice BRMs think of themselves as account managers, whose job is to make sure the needs of business partners are routed to the proper people in the IT organization. This is a dreadfully limited role. Sooner or later, someone is going to wonder why such seasoned, skilled resources are adding so little value.
   - **The BRM role is not an account manager.** BRMs, like boxers, fight for themselves. They understand the stakes, and work every day to prove their worth.
3. **Gap Filler.** Weak BRMs are victims of dysfunctional IT organizations, stepping in to fill any and all gaps in the needs of their business partners that are not being adequately met by the IT organization.
   - **The BRM role is not a gap filler.** BRMs understand that their role is larger than gap-filling, and that one way to meet the needs of their business partners is to become more involved in partnering with the business to define long-term strategies that address the root-cause of core issues.

Glitches, Gulches, and Gotchas

It is important to realize that BRM is often a role that wields significant influence (personal power) but actually has little or no authority over any of the many individuals and groups necessary for the efforts of BRMs to pay off (positional power). For example:

> *BRM is often a role that wields significant influence but actually has little or no authority*

- **The Service Management Glitch.** If basic IT services (email, help desk, mobile support) are less than excellent, the business partner is going to complain. This begins a vicious cycle. The BRM intervenes, using relationships and relationship skills to escalate and defuse the problem, and pulls off a minor miracle. Two bad things follow:
    1. The problem is solved though heroics. Heroes are celebrated, and the idea that heroes keep the lights on and the trains running on time (metaphorically speaking) gets reinforced.
    2. Business partners begin to see the BRM as the go-to person for IT operational problems. When BRM representatives are not invited to the metaphorical strategy table, the reason is clear. Why would anyone invite the janitor to help formulate strategy? (With all due respect to the hard working and effective janitors out there.)
- **The Solution Delivery Gulch.** If solutions delivery does not perform with excellence, meeting never-ending business demand, delivering solutions that work the first time, on time and within budget, then anything the BRM does to stimulate and surface demand is going to backfire.
- **The Maintenance and Break-Fix Gotcha.** If solutions maintenance is not responsive, proactive, and prescient, and business processes are interrupted, BRM is going to get dragged into the tactical fray, and lose its license to be strategic in the future.

Emergent BRM Success: An Example

A typical scenario of emergent BRM success is that the CIO begins to notice that the relationship with supply chain has improved by leaps and bounds over the last couple of years. The CIO recognizes that the ERP deployment, painful as it was, is now through the worst, and is starting to deliver on its supply chain improvement promises.

At the same time, the CIO keeps hearing positive messages about Samantha—the IT executive who led the supply chain ERP implementation, She seems to be spending a lot of time with the supply chain business teams. The CIO knows the business partners love Samantha, and that she is clearly seen as their champion and the go to person for things related to (and sometimes unrelated to) supply chain IT.

The CIO, realizing that Samantha is managing the IT-supply chain relationships, thinks: "Bingo. Samantha is acting in the role of Business Relationship Manager. Maybe I need to formalize the BRM role and appoint more people like her to fill it."

More Subtle Sources of BRM Failure

In many respects, the bullet points above are obvious—though that does not make them uncommon or easy to deal with—but there are also more subtle unintended consequences that face BRMs.

Will the real master of the BRM please stand up? *The general rule is that the BRM represents IT to the business and the business to IT. It is a bridging role. Sounds good. Makes sense. But when push comes to shove—as it will sooner or later—it is important to know where the allegiance of the BRM will really lie. This is not an insurmountable challenge, but it is one that can test even the strongest of relationship skills.*

Which business unit really rules? *Typically there are several, sometimes dozens, and occasionally a hundred or so BRMs, each representing some business unit, or process, or geography, or even a mix of these. BRMs not only balance business and IT issues, they also collectively balance issues among and across business units, capabilities, and processes. In theory, Business-IT governance—as a tool of a robust enterprise strategy and architecture—does the heavy lifting in terms of balancing these forces. In practice, however, there is the ever-present company politics, and the inevitable forces of self-interest, survival, and squeaky wheels. The ability of the BRM to surface these disconnects, and to manage the executive sponsors becomes a key factor in future success.*

Management wants BRM to get involved in labor negotiations? *Being a successful BRM tends to bring a healthy dose "of be careful what you wish for". Successful BRMs are seen as valued members of the business leadership team (as well as valued members of the IT leadership team). Sooner or later, however, these BRMs will be expected to get involved in things outside their scope or domain of expertise. On the one hand, this a sign that BRM has arrived. On the other hand, arriving provides many opportunities to set out on a variety of other journeys. Not all of these journeys will make sense. Just saying "no" wears thin quickly, and seats at the strategy table can be lost much more quickly than they can be earned. Picking and choosing opportunities to participate, and having a graceful and constructive way of deflecting requests that don't make sense, becomes an additional core competency for successful BRMs.*

BRM has gone native. *At some point, the risk surfaces that BRM is disenfranchising the rest of the IT organization from the business, making IT staff appear to be commodities. This is when the allegiance of a BRM is most likely to be challenged—not only by IT peers but by business partners. And this is also when BRM roles and alliances must be carefully clarified.*

Common Business Relationship Management Failure Modes

There are multiple reasons that BRM can fail. Here are six of the most common failure modes and lessons learned about how best to address them.

BRM Failure Mode #1

Failure to Convince Senior Management of BRM Value

A common situation is for BRM to fail before it even gets started. People see the dysfunctions between the IT organization and its business partners, find industry references to the BRM role, and unsuccessfully wage a campaign to sell the need for this role to the CIO. There can be a couple of root causes behind this mode of failure:

1. The business case for the BRM role is not compelling to those who must approve it—a weak business case.
2. The person selling the business case has failed to deliver the case in a convincing manner—weak communications in terms of influence and persuasion.

Summary of Common BRM Failure Modes	
Failure Mode	*Recommended Approach*
1. *Failure to convince senior management of BRM value*	*Create a compelling business case to help the organization do more with less, and deliver the business case in a convincing and compelling way.*
2. *BRM as dumping ground*	*Be proactive in defining and clearly communicating the BRM role, including strategic implications and ways it helps to drive business value.*
3. *Strategic BRM when tactical BRM is needed*	*Don't try to foster new strategic partnerships and surface new and valuable business demands through BRM until the ability of the IT organization to supply basic services is no longer in question.*
4. *Tactical BRM when strategic BRM is needed*	*When the context requires strategic BRM, choose BRMs with experience and competencies to act as true strategic partners.*
5. *Total focus on the business partner at the expense of key IT Stakeholders*	*Build strong partnerships with both business and IT stakeholders as a way to align and converge business and IT capabilities.*
6. *BRM as single point of contact*	*Position BRM as a single point of focus.*

Lesson #1: Help the Organization Do More With Less

IT organizations are under constant pressure to do more with less. Staff, especially senior resources, are a large part of an IT budget, and head count is a closely watched metric. Often this means that hiring a handful of BRMs (or moving a handful of people into the BRM role) implies that people filling other roles must be replaced or back-filled. After several rounds of downsizing or rightsizing, there is no fat to be trimmed, and nobody wants to give up current roles and positions.

For this reason, the business case for BRM must demonstrate enough value to justify the cost and headcount associated with the role. The business case must then be presented in a manner that convinces leadership that the BRM role can be useful in optimizing the use of scarce resources while driving business value.

BRM Failure Mode #2
BRM As Dumping Ground
This happens when the BRM becomes a catch-all for requests that nobody else wants

Doing More With Less: Lessons Learned From Recessions
One clue to successfully doing more with less can be found in previous recessions. With over 30 years of management consulting under my belt, I've been through several major recessions. During these periods, much consulting activity is about taking cost out of the IT budget. I've learned several lessons through this work:

- *Conversations about cost lead to more conversations about cost ad infinitum. IT will never be cheap enough if all management does is focus on cost. The key is to shift the conversations to value.*
- *Conversations about business value realization have a huge impact on demand. Low value demand can be suppressed, making room for higher value possibilities. In any portfolio analysis there will be some variation on the Pareto Principle. 80% of IT projects will deliver just 20% of the total realized business value. Reducing activities on low value demand is a wonderful way of freeing up resources and budget for higher value activities.*
- *Business value conversations result in more value conversations. Freeing up resources that are working on low value activities makes space for higher value activities, and that is exactly what the BRM role is about: surfacing, shaping and satisfying demand based upon business value.*
- *Many costly IT assets are under utilized. The pursuit of the next shiny object tends to add significant IT cost, often without creating significant new value. Better leverage of an existing, funded asset is a great way to create value without adding significant cost.*

to deal with, or for requests that don't have a clear owner. Lack of organizational clarity is usually a root cause. This failure mode may occur when the BRM role is announced without a clear definition of its purpose.

Others in the IT organization fear that the BRM might invade their territory, but also see it as an opportunity to get rid of tasks they don't like (or feel that someone else should be doing.) So at every opportunity, requests get deflected to the BRM: "Oh, our BRMs take care of that kind of thing. Here is an email address and phone number."

Lesson #2: Organizational Clarity is BRM's Biggest Friend

It is essential for organizations to be proactive in defining the BRM role with all its strategic implications and ways BRM helps to drive business value. It is important to reinforce the strategic, value creating purpose for the BRM role in day-to-day behaviors.

> *It is essential for organizations to be proactive in defining the BRM role with all its strategic implications and ways it helps to drive business value*

- Take time to work with key stakeholders on the IT side to define rules of engagement and interaction models.
- Take some use cases, and work through the solutioning life cycle from idea to retirement. Identify which roles are engaged, when they are engaged, and how they are engaged.
- Define high-level SIPOC (supplier, inputs, process, outputs, customer) models.
- Ensure comprehensive understanding and buy-in from business partners and IT stakeholders.

BRM Failure Mode #3
Strategic BRM When a Tactical BRM Is Needed

This is a very common BRM failure mode. Here is one scenario. For whatever reason, the IT organization is seen to be not fully satisfying the demands and expectations of its business partners.

In response the IT organization undertakes some type of transformation. The initiative often has several aspects, such as deployment of a service management framework, operating model realignment, process management program, sourcing strategy, and deployment of a BRM role/capability.

One or more individuals are nominated to lead the BRM deployment. They do their research, perhaps retain some consulting advice, build a team and, with high hopes and a strong sense of damn the torpedoes, they create and execute a BRM deployment plan.

All this sounds reasonable, but the disconnect is that the vision of BRM to be deployed is that of a strategic relationship between the IT organization and business partners. The BRMs chosen to fill the role are relatively senior people. They are well-qualified to work with senior business executives with a focus on business demand shaping and business value re- alization. Meanwhile, service manage-

> *When multiple changes are going on simultaneously, performance degradation can take time to resolve*

ment, operating model realignment, outsourcing, and other initiatives are underway. When multiple changes are going on simultaneously, performance degradation can take time to resolve.

This is similar to the dilemma a golfer faces who is not only working on a new swing, but is also using radically new clubs and a revolutionary new ball, is wearing inno- vative, experimental golf shoes, and is playing on a brand-new course. The golfer, determined to improve a golf swing, knows that the improvement initiative will likely be accompanied by performance setbacks.

While the new BRM team is trying to foster new strategic partnerships, and is surfac- ing new and valuable business demands, the ability for the IT organization to sup- ply even basic services is seriously compromised. This is especially true at the start of major new outsourcing arrangements which can take a year to eighteen months to stabilize.

Business partners quickly lose patience as current services falter, and newly surfaced demands get placed in backlog. It does not take long for one or both of two situations to materialize:
1. BRMs get dragged into tactical fire fighting. This is OK, but once BRMs are per- ceived as tactical resources, it may be hard for them to reposition themselves back into the strategic role they were originally intended to fill.
2. The benefit of the BRM role is marginalized by the perception that BRM is not add- ing value, especially when BRM resources are senior and relatively expensive.

Lesson #3: Don't Position BRM as Strategic When the Context Demands a Tactical BRM

It is difficult to migrate from tactical to strategic BRM. It is more effective to position BRM as adding strategic value from the start. This is especially true when BRM resources are senior and relatively expensive.

BRM Failure Mode #4
Tactical BRM When a Strategic BRM Is Needed
This is less common than Failure Model #3 above, but it still occurs—especially when an organization has blindly followed a framework (like ITIL) without a sufficient understanding of the supply maturity context. Here is a scenario.

The IT organization has implemented a service management framework such as ITIL, where the need for a BRM role is recognized. Some people from the service management function are appointed to BRM roles and deployed. The service management initiative has been effective, so the metaphorical lights stay on, and trains run on time.

After a while, business partners let IT management know that BRMs don't add much value. Since things seem to work OK, having tactical people in the BRM role seems like unnecessary overhead.

Sometimes it is IT management that comes to the conclusion that the BRM role has served its purpose and abandons it. Meanwhile, there is little to no improvement in the business value that is realized from investments in IT capabilities. All the basics work well, the business orders (mostly) get taken care of, but there is a sense of general disappointment in IT's strategic and innovation capabilities.

Lesson #4: Don't Position BRM as Tactical When the Context Demands a Strategic BRM
Tactical BRMs help keep the lights on, and the trains running on time, but once those table stakes have been achieved, the tactical BRM will (to extend the metaphor) run out of steam!

Someone with the competencies and authority to be a strategic BRM can operate at a tactical level, but someone without those competencies cannot operate at a strategic level. It is very difficult to migrate purely tactical BRMs to a strategic role.

It is very difficult to migrate purely tactical BRMs to a strategic role

They are unlikely to have the experience, gravitas, and competencies to act as a true strategic partner, or to be granted the executive level access they need to be successful in the strategic BRM role.

BRM Failure Mode #5

Total Focus on the Business Partner at the Expense of Key IT Stakeholders

This trap is easy to fall into when new BRMs see their business partners as their main clients and focus of attention. If BRMs understand that their true mission is to help

Need for a Single Point of Focus

I recall interviewing a business executive about his needs and expectations from his IT organization. He said, "The last time I needed to talk about a possible new IT solution, I set up a meeting with my new Business Relationship Manager. Seven people from IT came to that meeting. We had to find a conference room and move the meeting. By the end of the meeting, most of those present had said nothing, but they had all furiously taken notes, presumably each capturing the same things. No wonder IT costs too much and delivers too little."

Too Many Cooks

It's a familiar situation. One that is understandable but not acceptable. I imagine the seven IT representatives at the meeting included the BRM, a couple of business analysts, an enterprise architect, project manager and a couple of subject matter experts. They all wanted to be there so nobody would miss anything. Perhaps they thought a show of force would impress the business partner when, in fact, it had the opposite effect.

Too Many Specialists

Yes IT is complicated stuff and, ultimately, you have to get it right. 80% availability is not adequate for most IT solutions. This has led to an IT world that is full of specialties. Specialization is fine. But do all the specialties need to be represented in an initial meeting with the client? How are the client's needs best handled in terms of IT relationships? How can we create an exceptional experience for our client?

The Need for a Single Focus of Contact

The needs of both the business group and the IT organization are best served when there is a single focus of contact: an individual who shepherds all substantial contacts between business and IT. This is one of the roles of the BRM. In this role they are not a single point of contact (SPOC), but they do own the Business-IT relationship. This means they are accountable for the success of that relationship. As such, they need to be aware of all contacts between business and IT.

So if I'm an enterprise architect, and I run into a business executive in a corridor and he mentions some specific need or IT issue, it is my responsibility to let the BRM know. Similarly as a BRM, if I hear something through my business relationship that the enterprise architect should be aware of, it is my responsibility to let the architect know.

that partner increase the business value they are extracting from investments in the IT organization's capabilities and assets, this is where BRMs should spend the majority of their time. Supporting the business partner is a key function. However, it is only part of the BRM role.

Often when the BRM role is first introduced, key stakeholders in the IT organization fear that they have been disenfranchised. They might feel that their business facing activities are the most important (or enjoyable) aspects of their job, and might (wrongly) assume that those business facing activities are going to be curtailed (or even eliminated) by the new BRM role.

Lesson #5: BRMs Need to Build Strong Relationships With Key IT Stakeholders

The mission of the BRM role is to first align, then converge, business and IT capabilities. To achieve that, BRMs need strong partnerships with both business and IT stakeholders. They must be able to skillfully navigate through the IT organization, and orchestrate the use of IT resources in the delivery of value to their business partners. At the same time, it is important that BRMs not focus on business partners to the exclusion of key IT stakeholders.

To be effective, the BRM must act as a bridge between IT and business partners. Bridges have to join both ends, otherwise they are bridges to nowhere.

> *To be effective, the BRM must act as a bridge between IT and business partners*

This role demands a strong partnership with key stakeholders on the IT side, otherwise the BRM cannot be an effective bridge.

BRM Failure Mode #6
BRM as Single Point of Contact

This is a common mistake that occurs when a BRM is positioned as the single point of contact between an IT organization and its business partners. The single point of contact role is often introduced in response to a common symptom—the business partner is unclear about who to contact for what. In other words, the root cause is lack of organizational clarity. The false belief is that by appointing a BRM as a single point of contact, the organizational dysfunctions arising from lack of clarity will be mitigated.

This can be a problem for several reasons:

1. **As a single point of contact, BRMs quickly become overwhelmed.** If they are effective at fielding calls, they will be called on more and more frequently, until they collapse under the weight of an ever-expanding list of questions to answer, and is-

sues to solve. If they are not effective at fielding calls, they just add to the dysfunction, and further alienate their business partners.

2. **BRMs quickly get dragged into tactical issues.** BRMs in a tactical role are unable to add real value and, sooner or later, they are seen as overhead. (By focusing solely on the tactical, they indeed become largely overhead.)

3. **The single point of contact role tends to alienate key stakeholders on the IT side.** Enterprise architects, strategic planners, portfolio and program managers, and business analysts value their access to their business partners. They resent having to negotiate with the BRM doorkeeper in order to gain that access.

4. **The single point of contact role addresses a symptom, not the root cause.** A lack of organizational clarity remains. With or without BRMs, this leads to inefficiencies, poor communications, dropped balls, and a chaotic, stressful work environment.

Lesson #6: Position the BRM as a Single Point of Focus
It is more beneficial to position BRMs in the role of single point of focus, helping connect to, and orchestrate, key IT roles, and establish individual BRMs as the relationship owner for the business partners they serve.

Relationship ownership carries certain responsibilities and accountabilities. It also must be afforded certain commitments by other key IT stakeholders. A primary commitment should be to keep the BRM, as relationship owner, informed about any contact or activity with the business partner.

Ownership of the Business-IT Relationship
A good model to consider is the one followed by many large consulting firms. They typically operate within rules of engagement whereby each client or prospect is owned

Questions Around Ownership of the Business-IT Relationship
Questions around the ownership of Business-IT relationships are intriguing for several reasons:
- *Ownership is an illusive term in this context. Just what does it mean to own a relationship?*
- *There are at least two sides to any relationship. It is important that all parties see the relationship in the same way. If you own the relationship with me, do I recognize that and behave accordingly? Do I need to?*
- *Context is everything. What works well for one company or one situation might not work at all for another. What works for your organization?*

by a specific partner. If someone other than that partner has contact with the client or prospect (which is absolutely acceptable), that person must ensure that the partner is made aware of the contact.

This is a common courtesy, both to the partner who owns the relationship, and to the client. It is also a means to ensure an efficient, transparent client relationship. More importantly, it fosters strong relationships, and a deep client knowledge.

To Whom Should Business Relationship Managers Report?

Here is a scenario posed by leadership: "We are evaluating a strategy to centralize IT, and implement Business Relationship Management (BRM) roles as part of centralization. Should BRM report to a centralized IT organization, should it report directly to the CIO, or can it be effective reporting to a level (or two) below the CIO?"

The most common reporting relationship for successful BRMs is directly to the CIO, but it is not the only one. In some cases the BRM has a dotted line relationship to the senior business executive for the unit they represent. In other cases, the BRM role is solid line to a senior business executive, and a dotted line to the CIO.

There are several factors to consider when answering the question of the BRM reporting structure.

Rule #1. Reporting Lines Are Weak Determinants of Success for the BRM Role

Reporting relationships are a very weak determinant of success for the Business Relationship Manager (BRM) role. Far more important are the competencies (especially business knowledge and re-

Reporting relationships are a very weak determinant of success for the BRM role

lationship skills) of the BRMs and the maturity of the business executives they partner with.

Rule #2. Heft Matters.

Notwithstanding Rule #1, the heft of the BRM role—the weight and implied authority it carries—does matter. One reason for this is that BRMs are often (either explicitly or implicitly) on a CIO succession path. They have skills and wherewithal to be a CIO in the future. For this reason, the BRM role may be seen as a developmental step. This has implications when choosing individuals to fill BRM roles, and for defining career paths.

> ## Business Relationship Manager Titles
> *Here is a question I hear from time to time: "My BRM organization is going through leveling and restructuring. I have several BRMs reporting to me and am working with very senior business executives with billion-dollar business units. My peers in the IT organization have Vice President titles because they have larger organizations than mine. My BRMs sometimes feel that their titles put them at a disadvantage when engaging with their business partners. Is this a common issue? Any suggestions for approaching this issue?"*
>
> *This is an interesting and relatively common dilemma. CIOs have faced issues about salary levels for years. They are often seen as having too many specialists, too many salary bands, and being out of step with the rest of the company they support.*
>
> *Exacerbating this, IT organizations often continue to equate the importance of a leadership position (and therefore level of that position) with the number of people in a given leader's organization. This is, of course, a false premise.*
>
> *Importance should have more to do with the nature of the leadership position rather than the number of folk reporting to that position. This is not only an invalid indicator of importance, but also drives dysfunctional behavior (i.e., organization size equals power).*
>
> *Steps for approaching this issue may include:*
> 1. *Identify key stakeholders in effecting a change to BRM titles/levels at the same time including human resources as a key stakeholder.*
> 2. *Identify what is in it (the WIFMs) for each stakeholder by determining:*
>   * *Problems resulting from and/or opportunities missed due to the current approach to BRM titles/levels*
>   * *Benefits anticipated from a future state with better-aligned BRM titles/levels.*
> 3. *Consider moving BRMs into the business units they represent.*
> 4. *Identify the optimal first steps in effecting meaningful changes to BRM titles/levels.*

The story a CIO should tell business executives when establishing the BRM role is along the lines of: "I am giving you one of my senior staff members to help surface, shape, and manage IT demand so that you get the highest possible value from IT investments and assets. In return for this gift, I expect you to treat this BRM as a member of your management team."

Rule #3. Context Matters.
There are many other contextual factors to consider here, including:

- What is the scope of the BRM role? Is it primarily demand management (shaping, surfacing and managing business demand for IT)? Or does the role include supply management, service management, or other responsibilities?
- Do the BRMs act as project or program managers for major initiatives?
- Do the BRMs sit on governance bodies, such as portfolio management or service management?
- How do BRMs engage with the supply side?
- How do they engage with enterprise architects?
- How mature is IT supply?
- How mature is business demand?

Access and Influence Are Key BRM Requirements

Access and influence are earned by BRMs through skills and behaviors, not because of title. Very young and relatively low-level BRMs can wield enormous influence, and can gain access to the highest levels of business executives as a result of their skills and abilities.

Some roles carry more weight than others, regardless of the number of people working in that role. In enterprises that are very hierarchical in nature, titles carry significant meaning. A BRM with the title of manager might find it impossible to get on the calendar of a vice president, while a director or another vice president may have ready access.

In hierarchical organizations, it is important for BRMs to leverage their influence and persuasion skills and their knowledge of business transition management principles (also known as principles of organizational change management).

In many organizations, contemporary management thinking and leading HR practices have helped flatten organizations and, thereby, have helped to negate the paradigm that the size of an organization is equal to its power.

Driving Business-IT Convergence 6
Through Business Relations

Business-IT convergence is a consequence of the evolution of IT which is simultaneously becoming increasingly ubiquitous, accessible, and capable

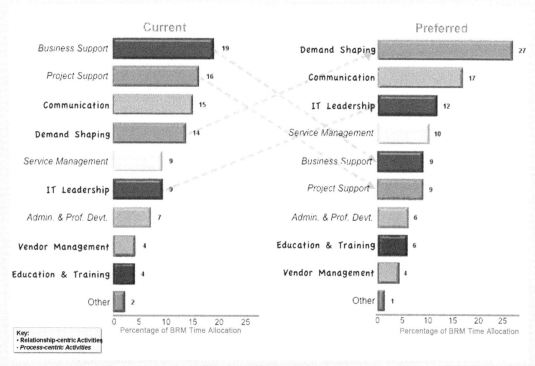

How BRM Time Allocation Changes from Current to Preferred

The BRM role is a result of the need for an efficient, effective, value-driven bridge between a service supplier and its business partners

Overview

This Chapter examines what the future may hold for Business Relationship Management, and the BRM role in fostering Business-IT convergence and stimulating business innovation. It examines BRM time allocation today, and compares this to what BRMs believe their time allocation should be going forward. It looks at the notion of the BRM team and shares some thoughts on measuring BRM impact.

Driving Business-IT Convergence Through Business Relations

What The Future Holds for Business Relationship Managers

To gain insight into the future of the BRM role, it is important to consider the mega-trend forces acting on the BRM role.

1. The BRM role is a result of the need for an efficient, effective, value-driven bridge between a service supplier (often an internal IT organization) and its business partners. BRM acts as a window in the wall through which IT-speak and business-speak are translated into each other, with the result that there is congruency between business demand for IT services, and the supply of those services based upon the potential for business value realization.

2. The consumerization of IT, and the availability of cloud-based services for software, infrastructure, and platforms (SaaS, IaaS, PaaS) are breaking down Business-IT barriers.

These forces were, in many ways, predicted by author and futurist Alvin Toffler who wrote about the separation between production and consumption that helped fuel the industrial revolution. Toffler suggested that the technologies of the *Third Wave* would heal that breach with a rise of *prosumerism*—the combining of production and consumption.

When applied to the IT provider-consumer relationship, this shift can be thought of as the *convergence of business and IT*.

Predicting the future is always a dangerous proposition. However, a close look at the dynamics of these forces may lead to the conclusion that the BRM role is a temporary one that will eliminate the need for itself over time.

Broaden BRM Influence, Not the BRM Team

I was leading a Business Relationship Manager (BRM) class and we got into a great discussion about how many BRMs are needed. This is always a difficult question because the answer begins with, "It depends."

I suggested a thought experiment to the class: Imagine this scenario. Your BRM team is doing amazing things. Business Value Realization has significantly increased and business executives recognize this achievement. They attribute the stunning results to Business Relationship Management and to the tools, techniques and skills the BRMs have brought to bear.

The question is: Should you increase the size of the BRM team because they are so effective or should you decrease team size because you no longer need as many?

One of the class participants thought for a moment and responded with, "I think you should work to broaden your influence and reach rather than expand the BRM team."

Perfect! In some respects, I believe that successful BRMs work hard to eliminate the need for their role. For example, they help their business partners and provider stakeholders develop and strengthen their own capabilities. In my experience people who work themselves out of a job always have full employment. They grow in their own capabilities and rise up through the ranks.

BRMs will do well to approach their role as though it is indeed temporary by adopting a *teach them to fish* philosophy rather than a *feed them* model. By following this approach, the BRM role tends to evolve as a way to remain relevant and is, therefore, valued well into the future.

Driving Business-IT Convergence: The Evolving BRM Role

Some would say that the purpose of the BRM role is to improve alignment between business and IT. This is a flawed notion. The alignment issue has been present since the earliest days of computing, and the problem can't be fixed by trying to close the alignment gap. Instead, resolving the alignment issue requires a very different perspective—one of driving Business-IT convergence. (To paraphrase Albert Einstein: Today's problems can't be solved with yesterday's thinking.)

Business-IT Alignment

Alignment can refer to strategy, and the degree to which IT strategy and business strategy are aligned. Alignment can also refer to structure. IT capabilities are structured to align with business structures and needs. But there's a crucial third leg to the Business-IT alignment stool. That is the alignment of relationships that sit between business units and IT capabilities. Mutual understanding results in Business-IT alignment. When there is excellent mutual understanding among key stakeholders, businesses and their IT organizations become aligned.

Alignment is, by its very nature, always retroactive. When business strategy changes, IT has to respond to those changes. When new IT capabilities are created, business strategy has to determine how to take advantage of those capabilities. The forces acting on both the business and the IT organization impact the dynamics of mutual understanding. Over time it can become nearly impossible to keep business and IT in alignment.

Business-IT Convergence

Business-IT convergence is a consequence of the evolution of IT which is simultaneously becoming increasingly ubiquitous, accessible, and capable. Information and IT are embedded in nearly every aspect of business, industry, and government. With technology advances, the roles of IT professionals and business professionals increasingly overlap.

With technology advances, the roles of IT professionals and business professionals increasingly overlap

Today there are business professionals who have access to tools that let them accomplish more with technology in an hour than could be accomplished by yesterday's IT professional in a week. These are people who can be considered IT professionals in every respect but one. They don't work for an IT organization. Rather they are deeply embedded in the business.

This is Business-IT convergence and it shows up in many ways. The consumerization of IT which is blurring the line between corporate and personal technology is one aspect of convergence. At the same time, the nature of corporate IT is fundamentally changing as roles that were traditionally embedded in the IT organization are now formally embedded in the business. This has major implications for IT infrastructure, for uses of cloud computing, and for the IT operating model which must now be defined as an aspect of the entire enterprise, not just the IT organization.

Empowerment Results in Business-IT Convergence

When the business is empowered with information, and IT provides a robust infrastructure coupled with the knowledge and skills needed to drive value from IT, then convergence, and the type of alignment thus gained, is not only lasting, it actually strengthens and deepens over time. BRM is key to ensuring that the IT infrastructure is fully appropriate, and that the necessary knowledge and skills are in place to properly leverage it.

Value Through Relationships

In most organizations IT activities belong to an organization of IT professionals (e.g., corporate IT), while business value is realized in the business of the business. Many IT professionals protest that they are part of the business. While this is a noble position to take, and an appropriate aspiration, it is generally not the reality experienced by those in line positions dealing day-to-day with profit and loss.

Since the early 1990s, the Business Relationship Management (BRM) role has emerged, and has been formalized. In some respects, it appears as a hybrid of business line professional and IT professional, with the emphasis on business. The BRM role was primarily intended as a means of bridging the gap (or in some case the chasm) between IT organizations and their business partners, and better linking IT costs with business

Value-based Business Relationship Management

Much of my career has focused on the relationship between IT and realized business value. When I say "realized business value," I mean:

- *The executive management team fully recognizes IT value contributions and invests in IT infrastructure and capabilities with confidence in the return they will experience on those investments.*
- *The executive management team recognizes that the value contributed by IT is real and integral to business success, even though not all that value will show up directly in traditional accounting systems. They understand that not all business value is visible through generally accepted accounting practices (GAAP).*
- *The executive management team understands that business value is often a function of multiple initiatives with complex and often opaque cause and effect relationships. Sometimes these initiatives are connected via a program management structure but other times they are seemingly unrelated.*
- *The executive management team treats infrastructure investments as options from an investment and value management perspective. They appreciate that IT infrastructure investments typically do not create realized business value in and of themselves but rather they enable other investments that do create value.*
- *Most importantly the executive team understands, embraces and actively engages in the management of IT value realization. They share a vision of and a passion for Business-IT convergence.*

> ## Tactical Badge of Courage
> *I wish I'd had $10 for each BRM who has told me, "I don't have time to be strategic. Tactical demands consume all my effort and energy."*
>
> *Deeper assessment and reflection usually reveals that the lack of time to be strategic is self-inflicted. It is worn as a badge of courage to display how important the individual is to keeping the lights on and the trains running on time.*
>
> *If IT supply maturity is low (indicated by unreliable IT services or poor customer experience with IT) then tactical and operationally-focused BRM activities provide an essential foundation on which to build more value-based roles and capabilities.*
>
> *However, experience shows that the BRM role is more sustainable and has a greater positive impact on business value realization when it is strategically focused.*

value. The role comes in many variations, from a relatively tactical and operational focus, to one more strategically and business-value focused.

Understanding and Avoiding Value Detractors

Of all roles the BRM role seems to be most prone to being dragged in directions that are not seen to be valuable. There are several reasons for this:

1. **Urgency always seems to trump value.** BRMs who have not reached an agreement with key stakeholders on how the role can and should work to deliver the highest business value, are more likely to spend their days dealing with operational (and largely tactical) issues. These BRMs might feel like heroes at the end of the week, but their business partners and key IT stakeholders are less likely to see them in a heroic light.
2. **Any activity seems worthwhile when explicit outcomes are not defined.** It is easy to confuse busyness with effectiveness. In the heat of the moment these things can feel the same even when they are not.
3. **When people are under stress, they fall back on their core competencies.** BRMs who were successful project managers before taking on the BRM role are readily dragged into project management activities. This trap is easy to fall into. The focus on tactical activities, and the operational rewards that come with performing them, becomes an excuse for not having time to be strategic.
4. **BRMs sometimes feel compelled to collude with dysfunctional behavior.** For example, service management might be poorly implemented with a result that services are not clearly defined, service levels are erratic, and there is insufficient

transparency into how services work and how customers experience the services created. Rather than act as change agents to upgrade service management discipline, the BRM steps in to mask poor customer experience or respond to service failures. This enabling behavior might feel good to the BRM, but tends to make things worse over the longer term. It also limits the time available for the BRM to take on higher value activities.

Relationships Through Activities

Individuals have many types of relationships from casual and informal (e.g., Facebook friends and LinkedIn connections) to intimate and formal (spousal or employer-employee). These relationships are instantiated and developed through activities such as posting status to a social media site, celebrating an anniversary, and comforting a loved one in need. Similarly BRM activities can be categorized as two major relationship types:

BRM activities can be categorized in two major relationship types: relationship-centric activities and process-centric activities

- **Relationship-centric Activities.** These are activities that depend upon the customer-intimate nature of the BRM relationship with the business, and things that cannot be achieved effectively without that relationship.
- **Process-centric Activities.** These are activities that depend upon robust processes such as project management, program management, service management, and those associated with process frameworks such as ITIL and COBIT.

Relationship-centric Activities

There are five classes of relationship-centric BRM activities.

1. **Demand Shaping.** Identifying, surfacing, and assessing possibilities for using IT services and capabilities including strategy formulation, business/technology research, consulting, and increasing business knowledge about business value realization through technology
2. **Communication.** Proactively informing key stakeholders about things they need to know and, in turn, being informed by key stakeholders about things IT needs to know
3. **IT Leadership.** IT Leadership team meetings, and leading or participating in key internal IT initiatives (e.g., process improvement and transformation)
4. **Vendor Management.** Working with external vendors and service providers
5. **Education and Training.** Spending time in formal training (as opposed to training others)

Time Allocation Research: How BRMs Allocate their Time

In 2014 I conducted a research project on BRM time allocation. My goal was to find out where BRMs spend their time and where they believe they should be spending their time. (More recently I have used the same research instrument with consulting clients and found that data patterns have not changed significantly over time.)

The chart at the beginning of this Chapter (p. 111) illustrates an analysis of preliminary data collected in late September 2014 from forty BRMs located around the globe. Relationship-centric activities are shown in bold and process-centric activities are shown in italics. On the left side of the chart is how BRMs reported their current time allocation and on the right side is the ideal time allocation reported by BRMs. At the time of the survey over 75% of those who responded said they had more than one year experience in their role and one-third had more than three years experience.

Key Observations

BRMs reportedly spent over 50% of their time on process-centric activities. The top three activities are business support, project support and communication. Of these the top two activities are process-centric. Compare this with ideal time allocations identified by the BRMs. Ideally, the top three activities would be demand shaping, communication ,and IT leadership. This shift from current to ideal time allocation reduces BRM time spent on process-centric activities from 50% to 34%.

Key Takeaways from the BRM Time Allocation Research

- *The BRM role is most effective when it focuses on the customer-intimate value discipline for which it is optimized. Activities that are associated with the operational excellence discipline are better handled by IT operations, infrastructure, service management, business support, etc. When BRMs step into these operational activities, they may be masking deficiencies in operational capabilities. Of course BRMs must be involved in operational and infrastructure capabilities, but this should not represent the bulk of their allocated time.*
- *BRMs coming from an operational background must fight the tendency to step back into process-centric activities so they can keep focused on the more relationship-centric outcomes that the BRM role was designed to serve. BRMs often move into their role from more operationally focused roles. With operational experience as their comfort zone, they sometimes fall back into their operational core competencies then protest that they don't have time to be more strategic.*
- *Clarity of the BRM role and expectations are critical factors in BRM success. BRMs should collaborate with their business partners and key IT stakeholders to determine their most important activities and the expected time to be allocated to those activities.*

The lesson is: Don't squander expensive and scarce BRM time (and the valued time of business partners) on activities that don't depend upon relationship capital.

How BRMs Can Re-balance Their Time Allocation

The first thing BRMs must do to change their time allocation is to be aware of how their time is being spent and to classify it. They can then compare how they are spending their time against how the BRM team and their key stakeholders believe time should be spent.

A Simple 8-step Approach

1. *Review BRM relationship activity classification schema shown in the graph on p. 111. Customize the list to fit your context and environment.*
2. *Track your time by activity for one month. Do this for what you believe is a typical month.*
3. *Normalize the data for any cyclical or special factors.*
4. *Rank your activities by business value as determined by your business partners. This will, of course, be inherently subjective. In practice it will be nearly impossible to link realized business value with specific activities during a given month. Simply engaging your business partner in a dialog about what activities were the most value to them can be highly illuminating and inherently relationship building.*
5. *Rank activities by time expenditure and percentage of time spent on each activity.*
6. *Review the biggest gaps between activities your business partner believes are most valuable and your actual time allocation. Why are you spending time on activities that seem to create the least value? How can you eliminate or at least reduce time you are spending on these low-value activities? There may be some activities that your business partners rate as low-value that you cannot eliminate, for example, administration or performance management of others. But you may be able to find ways to reduce the amount of time you spend on these activities, or at least find ways to help your business partner understand why the activities may actually be valuable to them.*
7. *Validate your findings and conclusions with your business partners and reconfirm the changes you plan to make to how you spend your time. Be careful. You are setting expectations, so make sure they are realistic and that you will be able to live by them.*
8. *Execute your plan and monitor your time allocation against that plan. Periodically, repeat the exercise (for example, once every 6 months), engaging your business partner in the analysis.*

Process-centric Activities

There are four classes of process-centric BRM activities.

1. **Business Support.** Responding to requests supporting day-to-day needs associated with running the business, and the IT capabilities that support it. These activities exist due to IT service management deficiencies. They tend to be reactive and

largely unplanned. Although necessary, they often create little new business value.
2. **Service Management.** Providing key input to service management regarding service strategy, design, delivery, operations or improvement
3. **Project Support.** Performing activities associated with specific Business-IT projects (funded initiatives). Effective project management processes should reduce the amount of project support needed from BRMs.
4. **Administration and Professional Development.** Activities such as resource management, time recording, professional development of others (supervision, coaching, training others, performance management)

Shifting From Process-centric to Relationship-centric Activities

The primary purposes of the BRM role are to strengthen the Business-IT relationship and, through that relationship, shape and influence business demand, and increase the value the business realizes from IT.

> *The BRM role emphasizes relationship-centric activities*

The BRM role emphasizes relationship-centric activities because BRM is essentially about the customer-intimate value discipline. This is one of three value disciplines identified by Michael Tracy and Fred Wiersema in their seminal book, *The Discipline of Market Leaders: Choose Your Customers, Narrow Your Focus, Dominate Your Market (1997).*

In contrast, process-centric activities such as business support, project support and service management are best suited to organizations optimized for the operational excellence value discipline, where the emphasis is on robust processes and continuous improvement rather than strong relationships. Any time spent by BRMs on process-centric activities not only detracts from the relationship-centric activities but may actually mask process dysfunctions elsewhere in the IT organization.

Re-balancing BRM Time Allocation

As described in the case study on the following page, there is significant value in a thoughtful evaluation of where BRMs actually spend their time compared to idealized time allocation.

This exercise can lead to deliberate actions that will shift time allocation towards a more ideal pattern. (A simple 8-step approach to BRM time allocation re-balancing is provided on the facing page.)

Involving business partners in this analysis can reveal the needs and expectations of

BRM and Self-Organization: A Case Study

I led a mini-benchmarking exercise with two former clients with whom I had previously done extensive BRM training. The purpose of the benchmark was to find out how their BRM approach had evolved, what was working well and where the teams still had challenges. In both cases, the clients had converged on a Business Relationship Management teaming approach—essentially a set of business unit-facing Business Relationship Management teams comprising a very senior BRM (by any title), a solutions manager and an enterprise architect.

One Business Relationship Management team had formed naturally (i.e., nobody had told them how to organize). This team was in a fairly sophisticated client in an information intensive industry with an exceptional quality of IT leadership and management.

One of the BRMs met with a business architect and a solution manager. They decided they needed to set time aside to meet, talk, and strategize in order to present a cleaner, simpler face to the business partner. They wanted to be more deliberate and proactive in shaping business demand rather than simply responding to it. They saw the formation of the Business Relationship Management team as an experiment. They did not ask permission. They just went ahead and tried it. It was an inspiring story with impressive results.

I met with the Business Relationship Management team and other architects, BRMs and solution managers to talk about how to generalize the model and duplicate it for the BRMs in other business units and companies. We analyzed what had changed as a result of the Business Relationship Management team approach, both from the perspective of individual IT roles and from the business client's perspective.

The Business-IT interface is an extremely complex space. The Business Relationship teaming approach works at this client because it is organic and was emergent. It works because team members have mutual trust and respect. It is the role of the team that is important and brings the magic, not the roles of individual team members. They talk about having each other's backs covered and about the fact that client executives know that they can talk to any member of the BRM team and reach the whole team at the same time. Any Business-IT conversation quickly and automatically gains the perspectives of enterprise architecture, solution delivery and relationship management. Business executives don't need to be concerned about who to call for what, nor do they have to sit down with five IT specialists to get things done.

My question to the team was how to codify the approach and generalize it. The response from the Business Relationship Management team members was surprising and distressing on the one hand, yet obvious and comforting on the other.

Their counsel was this: "We formed into a team because we wanted to, not because we were told to. So don't try to codify this approach too much. It won't work."

the partners. At the same time, working with business partners in making the shift to a more value-focused time allocation can encourage relationship building.

After all, it is not just the time of a single individual that is being optimized. Shifting BRM activities from process-centric activities to relationship-centric activities also impacts how business partners make effective use of their time.

The Power of Self-Organization

Ralph D. Stacey in his great book *The Chaos Frontier* (1991) defines self-organization as a process in which the components of a system spontaneously communicate with each other, and abruptly cooperate in coordinated and concerted common behavior.

Viewing organizational spaces (such as the Business-IT interface) as complex systems operating at the edge of chaos (scientifically speaking) reveals such insights as:
1. Variety, randomness, paradox, information, and interconnection are sources of creativity.
2. Organization is a natural, spontaneous act. To force it to be otherwise is not sustainable or effective.
3. Systems have a capacity to self-organize to great effect when given the opportunity.

Everything known about complex emergent behavior suggests that for life forms—such as Business Relationship Management teams—to really work, they have to behave like living organisms with porous boundaries, guided by a common sense of mission and purpose that can be compared to a genetic code. They do not thrive when sealed off from their world by hard boundaries and deterministic rules.

The danger feared by the Business Relationship team described in the case study on the facing page was that an organizational consultant would take the model and create formal organizational charters, role descriptions, and competency models and, in so doing, squeeze the life out of the Business Relationship team concept. (The word *life* is used deliberately here).

Measuring Impact of Business Relationship Management Capability

Before diving too far into measurements, BRM teams need to get a clear definition of goals and expectations for the BRM from business partners and provider stakeholders. Teams must also

BRM teams need to get a clear definition of goals and expectations for the BRM from business partners

be clear on the purpose of the measurements they are planning to create. For example:

- How will teams use the data that are surfaced?
- Will data be used to recognize and reward, to motivate, or to drive improvement?

Gaining clarity on these things will help Business Relationship Management teams ensure role and performance clarity in the context of intended purposes and appropriate metrics.

Tenets of Business Value Measurement

There are a variety of challenges (many well-documented) with measuring business value. Some basic tenets of business value measurement include:

1. There are important intermediary steps between inputs (the cost of which is an important element of net value realized) and impacts (the business value actually experienced by key stakeholders). This is often referred to as a *value (or benefits) dependency network*.
2. Trying to determine how business value will be manifested, and how this manifestation will be tracked, and measured, is always illuminating—even if the resulting metrics aren't perfect.
3. Shifting the focus of BRM measurement to business value sends a very important message to the organization about what is really important, and why the BRM capability has been established.

Positioning Business Relationship Management as a Value Driver

Positioning BRM properly is crucial to getting on a meaningful path to success. Too often, BRM is positioned so low in the food chain that business partners—especially those in executive positions—don't care, and won't invest their time to engage.

> *Positioning Business Relationship Management properly is crucial to getting on a meaningful path to success*

When BRMs tell their business partners that the BRM team is there to improve service quality, the business partners will probably be mildly pleased. When BRMs tell them that BRM is there to help drive business value from information and IT services and solutions, the business partners may become excited.

Moving From Inputs to Impacts

It is a mistake to say confidently things like: "This project will create $X business value." The reality is more likely: "This project (and its inputs), the results of which

The Ultimate Measure of Success: Business Value Realized

One question I hear frequently is: "We're setting up a Business Relationship Management (BRM) Capability. How should we measure our impact?"

I typically respond by asking my questioner: "What were the primary reasons you decided to establish a BRM capability? In particular, what do your business partners want to see out of the relationship?"

The reaction to this relatively straightforward question is usually telling—first in the noticeable pause before they are able to respond, then in the fuzziness of their response. The cliché, "If you don't know where you are going any road will do" applies here. If you don't know why the BRM capability was established, you will have a hard time establishing metrics.

I firmly believe that Business Relationship Management exists to serve three important purposes:
1. *To stimulate, surface and shape business demand for a provider's products and services*
2. *To ensure that the potential business value from those products and services is captured, optimized and recognized*
3. *To shape the provider's products and services and ensure that they are optimized to meet the business value demand*

will depend upon Q infrastructure capabilities (more inputs), and R and S projects (yet more inputs), will enable T changes in business capability (outputs), which will increase sales effectiveness by U% within V months (outcomes), which will be worth W (impact) to the organization."

But actions trump words every time. Engaging business partners in the types of value-clarifying dialog outlined above is useful. Even if they don't know why Business Relationship Management has been established, they will have experienced the reason for BRM first hand, and they will tell others about the power of the BRM capability.

Sorting through the value dependency network from inputs to impacts sheds light on how business value is to be created, and how it can be measured. Of equal importance, it will suggest intermediary results that can be measured, and that may be critical leading indicators of the final impacts.

Sorting through the value dependency network can also lead to important outcomes, especially when that process includes input from key stakeholders:

- Stakeholders get clarification of the value dependencies, and what it will actually take to realize the business value being targeted.
- In gaining clarity, stakeholders also gain buy-in and commitment to the initiatives associated with moving from inputs to impacts.

BRM as the Missing Link in IT-enabled Business Innovation

Few would argue that IT enables business innovation through new types of products and services, transformed business models, and improved lives for customers, consumers, shareholders, employees, and citizens.

IT-enabled Innovation

When Sam Walton recognized the competitive advantage Walmart could gain by turning inventory into information, he experienced (and then acted upon) an insight that would innovate supply chain management for big box retailers and ultimately for retailing in general.

When Max Hopper's team at American Airlines recognized (and then acted upon) the power of yield management as a means of dynamically pricing airline seats based upon supply and demand, he created a competitive advantage that put promising low-cost airlines such as People Express out of business.

When Amazon's Jeff Bezos recognized (and then acted upon) the opportunities in reinventing online retailing for an exceptional customer experience, he created a new business that today captures a major share of retail business and continues to innovate products and services.

Stories such as these appear frequently, although not as frequently as one might hope. But smaller examples appear all the time. Domino's Pizza reversed its slumping performance in large part by making online ordering a cornerstone of its business model through its web-based tools such as voice ordering, Pizza Tracker, 3-D Pizza Builder, and Pizza Hero tools.

Key Success Factors of IT-enabled Innovation
I've been fortunate in my career to be involved in IT Management research and learn from many talented academics and practitioners. Ten years ago one multi-company research study into IT-enabled innovation highlighted three key success factors:
1. *A clear and compelling innovation intent*
2. *An effective channel and structures that bring together business need/opportunities with IT capabilities/possibilities*
3. *An effective process for filtering, refining, testing and deploying innovation opportunities*

BRM Techniques for IT-enabled Innovation

Techniques for Demand Shaping

- *Value network analysis*
- *Scenario planning*
- *Appreciative inquiry*
- *Competitive intelligence*
- *Bibliometric analysis*
- *Capability gap analysis*

Techniques for Discovering Innovation Opportunities

- *Design thinking*
- *Brainstorming*
- *Knowledge café*
- *Synectics*
- *Why-why diagrams*
- *Behavioral prototyping*
- *Mind mapping*
- *Storyboarding*

Techniques for Deploying Innovation Opportunities

- *Design structure matrix*
- *Force field analysis*
- *How-how diagrams*
- *Stakeholder mapping and analysis*
- *Organizational change management*
- *Business experiments*
- *Rapid prototyping*
- *Agile development*

However, IT-enabled innovation has its limits. With the emergence of a wide range of innovation enablers such as the Internet of Things (IoT), inexpensive ways to identify and locate objects, people, and places, powerful analytical capabilities, wearable technology, agile methods, and smart phone apps, why does it seem that many businesses, government agencies, and organizations of all kinds, are stuck in the last century? Why does IT-enabled innovation always seem to refer to *over there*?

Skilled and properly positioned BRMs can help inject the success factors identified above. For example:

1. As a demand shaper, BRM helps stimulate the business appetite for innovation.

The skilled BRM uses techniques such as value network analysis, scenario planning, appreciative inquiry, competitive intelligence, bibliometric analysis, and capability gap analysis to help establish innovation intent.

2. As demand surfaces, the BRM discovers innovation opportunities using techniques such as design thinking, brainstorming, knowledge café, synectics, why-why diagrams, behavioral prototyping, mind mapping, and storyboarding.

3. With a focus on business transition and value realization, the BRM helps deploy innovation opportunities using techniques such as design structure matrix, force field analysis, how-how diagrams, stakeholder mapping and analysis, organizational change management, business experiments, rapid prototyping, and agile development.

Individuals in a BRM role can benefit by becoming knowledgeable in design thinking. To understand how innovation can create business value in context, questions can be asked such as:

- Where is innovation thinking taking place in the organization?
- How well connected is the BRM team with innovation thought leaders?
- How should BRM learn about innovation in the industry?
- How does the BRM team keep up with IT-enabled innovation?

This means truly understanding the business partner's business model, business processes, the marketplace, competitive strategies, and market forces. It also means knowing key stakeholders and influence leaders.

Razing Silos with Business Relationship Management

IT Organizations are complex organisms that have to adjust to rapidly changing, complicated ecosystems. They are fascinating places for organizational archaeologists and anthropologists to study, revealing layer upon layer of legacy architectures, organizing structures, artifacts, and sub-cultures.

While the technology IT manages changes quickly, methods and structures used to manage them take time to change

While the technology that IT organizations manage changes quickly, methods and structures used to manage them take time to evolve. These methods often develop more slowly than the end users who wish to adopt them would like. It takes time to learn how to manage a new computing environment—hence the importance of understanding Business-IT maturity.

Often by the time IT has learned how to manage an aspect of IT management (mainframe computing, security and integrity, for example) the world has moved on to other technologies (for example distributed computing), and technology specialists have to unlearn what they know, figure out how things must change, then introduce those changes into the environment.

Change often becomes messy when organizational change plans and intentions have to contend with real-world human factors such as change resistance, and the need to protect status, organizational power, and personal competencies.

BRMs and Organization Silos

One of the reasons the BRM role has emerged with a vengeance over the last few years is the creeping specialization within the enterprise IT domain. It can be said that BRMs act as business-facing generalists who help business executives and managers make sense of IT, and help IT organizations make sense of the businesses they support.

The Silo Trap

There are times when the specialists become so entrenched in their own empires that they have trouble engaging with BRM generalists (and with other specialist groups). BRMs sometimes face challenges related to these organizational silos.

> *BRMs act as business-facing generalists who help business executives and managers make sense of IT and help IT organizations make sense of the businesses they support*

Organizational silos often materialized in the distant past in response to changes in the work of the IT organization. Specialization also tends to lead to silos. Once silos are established, silo walls harden over time as a way to reinforce relevance and to protect those inside the silo from intruders. People in silos can be remarkably effective at defending their turf.

Examples of places silos can form include:
- Enterprise architecture
- Project and program management offices
- Business intelligence specialists
- Security specialists

The challenge is to break through silo walls. Probably one of the most important breakthroughs in organizational design since Frederick W. Taylor's book, *Principles of*

Scientific Management (first published in 1911), was the emergence of cross-functional teams. These teams bring together specialists such as design engineers, manufacturing engineers, and marketing specialists.

With this cross-discipline representation, linear, sequential processes become more parallel and iterative, shortening product development lead times, and improving product quality. The benefits of cross functional teaming can be achieved in IT organizations. (DevOps is a current example of cross-discipline teaming.)

The Trap of Siloed Transformation

Compounding the problem of organizational silos—and a clear indication of the resilience of silo mentality—many IT organizations engage in some form of transformation every few years (or when IT leadership changes).

The problem is, transformation initiatives are sometimes framed from within silos. Often the marching orders given to each member of the IT leadership team are: *Go forth and transform your organization*. In response to that command, the proverbial deck chairs on the Titanic are rearranged and, when everyone gets back to business as usual, the silos remain as entrenched as ever.

Breaching Silos from the Outside

To really soften silo walls requires a more holistic perspective, one that raises the question: *What is IT trying to do for its business partners?* They don't care about enterprise architecture or program management, or whatever. They are trying to drive business results by eliminating costs, innovating a product or process, or getting closer to their consumers.

BRM can be a significant force, bringing a holistic, external perspective, and orchestrating specialist groups to work together to help solve business problems.

Business Relationship Management with Teeth

Successful BRMs operate with just the right kind of hard edge needed to breach the silos. For a BRM to be a true change agent takes courage, leadership air cover, and a clear-minded vision of a better future. As Niccolo Machiavelli reportedly said: nothing is more difficult to undertake, more dangerous to manage, or more uncertain of success,

> *For a BRM to be a true change agent takes courage, leadership air cover, and a clear-minded vision of a better future*

than leading the introduction of a new order of things.

BRM and Cloud Services: Friends or Foes

Cloud computing is an important key to business innovation and a reality in most corporate computing environments today. Like it or not, it is an increasingly important part of the enterprise computing landscape. As discussed below, cloud computing is both a threat and an opportunity for BRMs.

Implications of Software as a Service

There are several important aspects of cloud computing, particularly in its Software as a Service (SaaS) variation. These include:

- Little to no capital outlay
- Low barrier to entry for the customer, typically communicated by vendors as: *sign a deal and you are in*
- Relatively attractive pricing
- Often, few decisions to make because what you see is what you get with little to no customization opportunities

SaaS reduces dependency on enterprise IT to find, evaluate, procure, operate, and maintain a business solution. While entry costs might be low, overall life cycle costs for SaaS solutions can be significantly higher than traditional IT solutions. (The typical business model for SaaS providers is to fully recover costs in four years. Revenues collected beyond that period are essentially pure profit.)

The danger is that business executives see SaaS as a business decision and sign up without involving their IT departments

The danger here is that with the attractiveness and ease of engaging SaaS services, many business executives see SaaS as purely a business decision, and sign up without involving their IT departments. Some will do this in ignorance of the wisdom and value of involving enterprise IT. Others will do it as an expedient measure in the belief that it is easier to ask forgiveness than to ask permission. The four aspects of SaaS outlined above have important implications.

Implication #1. The Funding Challenge

Depending upon the IT funding model, ongoing costs of SaaS solutions may well show up in the IT budget even though IT was not involved in the procurement decision.

As an analogy, it is as if the teenage son of a family took a second mortgage on the house to remodel his bedroom without asking permission of the parents, and put the new mortgage in the name of his parents.

Implication #2. The Architectural Challenge

The direct engagement of the SaaS solution by a business unit might lead to redundant or incompatible solutions. For example, business unit A might sign up for a learning management solution. Subsequently, business unit B decides to sign up for a second learning management solution.

The company now has two different learning management solutions leading to higher costs than if one solution had been shared. At the same time, the human resources organization now has a major headache when trying to manage staff development as an enterprise-wide initiative.

To continue the house analogy used above, the family teenage daughter now remodels her bedroom, and signs up with a different cable TV provider from the one procured by her parents. As a result, the parents now have two cable TV bills to pay.

Implication #3. The Data Analytics Challenge

As each business unit engages its own choices of SaaS solutions, disparate solutions fragment the overall data picture. The ability of the company to derive meaning from all the data that passes through it becomes more and more limited. The promise of big data collapses into the nightmare of *what data, whose data, and where did it come from.*

> *As each business unit engages its own choices of SaaS solutions, disparate solutions fragment the overall data picture*

Returning to the previous analogy, dad now has to hunt around to find out what TV channels are available in his house, and who is watching them.

Implication #4. The Wrong Problem/Wrong Solution Challenge

In many cases, business units that sign up for the SaaS solution may not have applied the necessary analytical skills and experience to understand the root cause of the business problem they are trying to address.

At the same time, an SaaS provider dealing with an unwary buyer may not have the business context, analytical skills or incentive to completely understand the business problem or to ensure that they (the provider) are giving the buyer the best possible solution.

It is as if the teenage children in this analogy are being sold high definition TV channels that won't work properly on their low definition television sets.

The Business Relationship Manager Solution

SaaS implications can be minimized when a skilled Business Relationship Manager acts as a bridge between business units and the IT organization, and works with SaaS providers to ensure the right problems are being solved in the most appropriate, cost effective, and efficient manner.

BRMs can help ensure that funding, architectural, and data management perspectives are all taken into account at the same time that they orchestrate the appropriate business and IT resources. These benefits of a well-implemented BRM role have existed for years. In the age of SaaS and cloud computing, the role becomes even more valuable.

The digital IT operating model applies to all aspects of IT across the enterprise.
Many elements of the model will be outside of the IT organization.

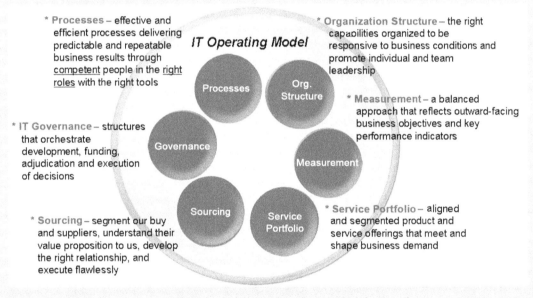

* **Processes** – effective and efficient processes delivering predictable and repeatable business results through <u>competent</u> people in the <u>right roles</u> with the right tools

* **Organization Structure** – the right capabilities organized to be responsive to business conditions and promote individual and team leadership

* **IT Governance** – structures that orchestrate development, funding, adjudication and execution of decisions

* **Measurement** – a balanced approach that reflects outward-facing business objectives and key performance indicators

* **Sourcing** – segment our buy and suppliers, understand their value proposition to us, develop the right relationship, and execute flawlessly

* **Service Portfolio** – aligned and segmented product and service offerings that meet and shape business demand

IT Operating Model

Processes · Org. Structure · Governance · Measurement · Sourcing · Service Portfolio

Elements of an IT Operating Model

A well designed and deployed IT operating model creates organizational clarity that smooths the wheels of IT capability.

Overview

This Chapter examines the concept of an IT operating model and the implications of the digital enterprise. It considers some principles for IT operating model transformation and how to differentiate between transformation and reorganization.

Transforming to a Digital IT Operating Model

IT Operating Models

"Do you need to have an IT operating model?" This LinkedIn group question led to an interesting discussion. One of the noteworthy aspects of the discussion was that several participants viewed an IT operating model as something optional that IT organizations may choose to have or not have.

All IT organizations have an IT operating model. It might not be well communicated or well understood across IT. It might be implicit rather than explicit. It might be badly broken. But every IT organization has an operating model or they would not be able to operate. The significant questions to ask about the IT operating model are:

- **Is it formalized** (i.e., has it been designed with deliberation, not just as an accident of bygone reorganizations)?
- **Is it effective** (i.e., does it consistently deliver what the business needs in the most effective ways)?
- **Is it efficient** (i.e., does it make the best possible use of assets and resources)?
- **Is it clear to all those who depend upon it** (i.e., do stakeholders and members of the IT organization understand it)?
- **Is it healthy** (i.e., is it continuously improving and sustainable)?

Beyond the Organization Chart

In many organizations the only explicit manifestation of the operating model is an organization chart. This is an incredibly limited (and limiting) way of expressing an operating model in any meaningful way.

The organization chart says who reports to whom but not what gets done or how it gets done. It says nothing about decision rights, key metrics or services. It says nothing

> ### Exploring an IT Operating Model for the Digital Enterprise
> *There are three key reasons to consider digital enterprise implications for IT operating models:*
>
> 1. *The types of IT products and services that must be delivered in a digital enterprise that fully exploits Web 2.0 are quite different from those in a Web 1.0 world.*
> 2. *The ways that IT products and services can be delivered in a digital enterprise are also quite different.*
> 3. *Designing and executing an IT operating model in a Web 2.0 context is also quite different from those in a Web 1.0 context.*
>
> *I'm actually most excited about point 3 above. It's something I've been exploring—both through multi-company research and through actual consulting engagements—and have found that Web 2.0 provides an incredibly powerful platform through which to design, actualize, and evolve an IT operating model.*

about needed competencies or rules of engagement between functions and groups.

Ownership of the IT Operating Model

This question of who owns the IT operating model can only be answered in the context of how ownership is defined. On one hand, it may help to think of the IT operating model as being owned by the IT leadership team, often with specific responsibilities allocated by domain (e.g., strategy, governance, delivery) to individual members of the IT leadership team.

On the other hand, if ownership of the operating model means who is responsible for the effectiveness of the IT Operating Model, the answer to this question is the CIO, with all operating model participants being responsible for the performance of their roles.

The IT Operating Model Is Not Just About the IT Organization

As business and IT converge, the IT operating model should be the model for all aspects of IT across the enterprise. Increasingly, many elements of the model will be outside of the IT organization, so there is an important aspect of business access to, and ownership of, the IT operating model.

For example, self-service guidelines and policies around *bring your own device* (BYOD) lend themselves to being part of the IT operating model.

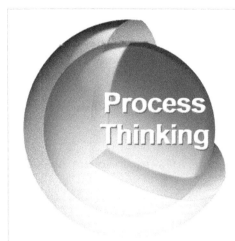

▷ **Consistency in approach**
▷ **Promoting transparency**
▷ **Leading to repeatability**
▷ **Enabling continuous improvement**
▷ **Ensuring higher quality**
▷ **Leading to improved relationships**
▷ **Resulting in increased realized value**

The Core of an Operating Model

Core of an IT Operating Model

Process thinking is at the heart of the creation of an IT operating model. An effective IT operating model should include processes that accomplish three things:

1. **Reduce confusion and noise** about the management of IT across a unit of analysis (e.g., company, division, enterprise)
2. **Consistently deliver what is demanded** by Business-IT strategy
3. **Be able to flex with changes** in demand or supply patterns

These accomplishments can be addressed through consistency in approach—which promotes transparency. This leads to repeatability, enables continuous improvement, and ensures higher quality. High quality leads to improved relationships with business partners which, in turn, results in increased realized value.

Components of An IT Operating Model

An IT operating model (shown on p. 135) is the basic framework that an IT organization follows to get its products and services into the hands of its partners. The primary elements are:

1. **Processes.** How to perform activities that deliver predictable and repeatable business results through competent people using the right tools. For example,
   - How is demand shaped?
   - How is demand surfaced and clarified?
   - How is demand turned into solutions that deliver intended (or better) business results?
2. **Governance.** How to make and sustain important decisions about IT. For example,

- How do business needs and initiatives get prioritized?
- How does IT manage the tensions between local and global optimization?
- How are standards chosen, and what are the consequences for deviations?
- How can flexible global sourcing be leveraged to achieve capability on demand?

3. **Sourcing**. How to select and manage the sources for IT products and services. For example,
   - How can the scale of IT be leveraged?
   - What work is done offshore, near shore, onshore, in house, in source, by contract?

4. **Services**. How the portfolio of IT products and services is defined. For example,
   - What is in the service catalog?
   - How are service levels managed and defined?
   - How are services differentiated by customer segment?

5. **Measurement.** How performance is measured and monitored. For example,
   - What are the shared goals of the IT organization?
   - How does the business determine value realized and delivered through IT investments?
   - How is IT improving over time?

6. **Organization.** How the IT organization is structured and organized. For example,
   - What capabilities should be located within the IT organization, and what can be within the business?
   - How does IT organize around major projects and programs?
   - How does IT organize around major products and platforms?

Note that organization (represented by the organization chart) is deliberately listed last.

How Web 2.0 Changes the Design of an IT Operating Model

With collaboration tools such as Wikis, social networks, and prediction markets, designing an IT operating model can be performed in a more collaborative and impactful way. It can be done so that the traditional artifacts of the design become living documents, collaboratively managed, and truly representative of the way work actually gets done.

With collaboration tools, designing an IT operating model can be performed in a more collaborative and impactful way

For example, process management (including all phases of process design, deployment, automation, work flow, and con-

> ## The Organization Chart and the IT Operating Model
> *For the last 50 years or so, IT operating model design was mostly an oxymoron. Operating models weren't designed so much as evolved through a series of random walk throughs.*
>
> *When deliberate design was attempted, it was typically though workshops with flip charts, post-its, PowerPoint slides, Visio diagrams, and so on. At the end of the day, there was an organization chart, organizational charters, templates, and process descriptions.*
>
> *Usually these were created as Word and PowerPoint documents that got emailed to and fro, edited, re-edited, eventually filed and never seen again until the next CIO and the next attempt to improve Business-IT alignment.*
>
> *For years when I consulted on IT operating model design, clients invariably wanted to start with the organization chart. I call that moving the deck chairs on the Titanic. It rarely solves anything.*
>
> *On the other hand, if IT teams work through the other elements (such as services, processes, and governance) the organizational decisions fall out relatively easily and far more coherently.*

tinuous improvement) are well-served by collaborative approaches and tools. Once a technology user is in a browser and on the web, the user has access to a wide range of collaborative tools that are helpful when performing process management work such as:

- Project management
- Mind mapping
- Polling
- Voting
- Training and communicating
- Financial modeling
- Drawing
- 3-D modeling

These collaboration tools, which are inexpensive and, in many cases free, can help create a productive work environment or even a process management toolkit for engineering an IT operating model.

The IT Operating Model Is Not Just About IT Processes
Although the focus here is on the design and deployment of IT operating models, the

> ## Documents: How Not to Deliver the IT Operating Model
> *Documents are an inefficient way to express operating models.*
> - *Documents create organizational confusion. Where is the document? Is this the latest version? Why is the content inconsistent with other documents?*
> - *Documents reinforce organizational silos. Who needs to know this? Who should own it? Who should review it?*
> - *Documents proliferate and deteriorate over time due to multiple changes that are hard to track, links that break, definitions and terms that become lost over time.*
> - *People are disinclined to read or use documents, especially at the moments of truth when they are most needed.*
>
> *Documents are also inefficient vehicles for engaging people in continuous improvement. That's why Wikipedia chose a Wiki as the ideal platform for engaging the world in its remarkable achievement of capturing human knowledge.*

same approaches apply to business process management for the digital enterprise. However, the IT organization is often well served *doing unto themselves* before they go too far *doing unto others*.

This is a matter of both need (i.e., IT organizations need a healthy dose of collaborative process management), and experience (i.e., IT organizations should gain some first-hand experience in the approaches before they plunge into business process management 2.0.)

The IT Operating Model Is Not Just About Web 2.0 Tools
While it is natural for IT professionals to gravitate towards tools for collaboration, collaborative approaches bring more than useful tools. Collaboration makes it much easier to follow agile methods, thereby delivering value sooner.

Collaboration brings issues of organizational and cultural change to the foreground. By bringing a broader selection of stakeholders into end-to-end process management, the challenges of process deployment, adoption, and ongoing refinement are significantly reduced. People are more engaged when they design, use, and improve processes they own.

IT Organization Design and the Value Disciplines
Value disciplines were first articulated in *The Discipline of Market Leaders (1995)* by Michael Tracy and Fred Wiersema. The authors describe three distinct value disciplines:
- **Operational excellence** means providing customers with reliable products or

services at competitive prices, and delivered with minimal difficulty or inconvenience.

- **Customer intimacy** means segmenting and targeting markets precisely, then tailoring offerings to match exactly the demands of those niches. Companies that excel in customer intimacy combine detailed customer knowledge with operational flexibility so they can respond quickly to almost any need—from customizing a product to fulfilling special requests.
- **Product leadership** means a focus on product innovation, offering products that push performance boundaries.

Experience shows that while any company has to be good at all three disciplines, operating models tend to optimize for one of these disciplines. Not everyone buys into this argument and, like all generalizations, there are some limitations to the assertion. Despite its detractors, this model has proven itself to be a valuable lens for operating model design over the years.

Translating this into the world of IT, it is clear that IT organizations have to embody all three disciplines. It is also interesting to note that the process of improving Business-IT maturity tends to focus on operational excellence needs first (IT infrastructure), then on the customer intimacy disciplines (business processes and applications), and finally on product leadership (business innovation).

IT operations (data centers, telecommunications, help-desks, etc.) lends itself to an operational excellence model. That is why frameworks, such as ITIL and COBIT, can be useful.

Discovery of IT-enabled opportunities demands customer intimacy

Discovery of IT-enabled opportunities demands customer intimacy, which is why this function is often best embedded in the business, and it is a focus of Business Relationship Management. Enterprise architecture and advanced technology R&D demand product leadership.

These functions work best with a central focus (perhaps a competency center, community of practice or center of expertise) coordinating a distributed network of subject matter experts.

For example, an architecture center of expertise owns the role of defining standards and enterprise-level models, but works through a network of business and technical

> ### Busting Silos with the Role Bomb!
> *Organization design (and by extension, operating model design) has traditionally been concerned with jobs as the primary unit of analysis—people working in fixed, dedicated positions with job descriptions. Within this context, there is a tendency to design operating models around jobs. This is a mistake.*
>
> *Let me illustrate this with an example. I was working with a client that was experiencing significant pain trying to implement a major enterprise system. One of the recurring issues was around the boundaries of responsibility between business operations groups and IT. With the new enterprise software that offered extensive user-configurable capabilities, the question was who should be responsible for what.*
>
> *It took them a while to understand the roles concept, and that roles can be distributed across organizational boundaries, but once they did, the problem was easily solved to the satisfaction of all stakeholders.*

architects distributed throughout the enterprise. These are roles, not necessarily full-time jobs.

The Emerging IT Operating Model

It is important to think of an IT operating model as an enterprise-wide construct of which the IT organization is but one component. Many more IT functions are being distributed and dispersed. Witness the so-called rise of *bring your own device* (BYOD).

Functions that were performed by a central IT group are being performed by the business individual. This move towards self-service and business embedded functions will only expand with emerging technology and capabilities such as business analytics and machine learning. As such, the IT operating model components can be thought of as comprising centralized, decentralized, and hybrid components. These might fall along the following lines:

Centralized Capabilities such as shared IT services. The value proposition is standardization and operational excellence through
- Enterprise architecture
- Enterprise shared infrastructure
- Enterprise shared solutions
- Security and privacy
- Sourcing and vendor management

Decentralized Capabilities such as business-dedicated IT services. The value proposition is customer intimacy and innovation through

- Business architecture
- Local and departmental solutions
- Business analytics

- **Hybrid Capabilities** such as networked IT services and communities of practice. The value proposition is integration and shared learning through
- Business-IT governance
- Value realization boards
- Innovation centers
- Organizational development and change leadership centers
- Business relationship and sourcing management
- Data visualization
- Integration
- Process management

Role or Job

Wikipedia defines role as a set of connected behaviors, rights, and obligations as conceptualized by actors in a social situation.

In the organizational (rather than social) setting, the concept of role is important for decoupling the rigid characteristics of job from organization. Roles when properly implemented, offer certain advantages compared with other design constructs.

Roles allow organizations to increase flexibility and agility as individuals take on multiple roles

Roles allow organizations to increase flexibility and agility as individuals take on multiple roles to suit the need at a given time under certain conditions, regardless of formal job description or position on an organization chart.

Roles can either be achieved or ascribed. An example of an achieved role is the *power PC user*. This is the person in the office who is something of a PC jockey (or MS Office Jockey or Excel whiz). This is the go-to person users contact when they need someone to help them figure out how to do something. Power PC users are not especially trained for this role. They are not formally compensated for it. It is not a function listed in their formal job description. Power PC users fill a role and are usually happy to fill it. At the same time, their colleagues are happy someone is available to assist them.

Similarly some organizations have the function of power user officially ascribed. In this case everyone knows that Mary is the ERP power user. For people who have questions or problems doing their jobs through ERP, Mary is the first point of contact. She may be able to answer their questions or, if not, she knows where to go to for an answer. She has been trained to be an ERP specialist. ERP support is part of her job, and she is accountable and often compensated or rewarded for it.

Breaking Down Silos With Roles

Roles fit in well with the shift from vertical to horizontal management and process-centricity. IT organizations attempting to transform to a more agile, flatter organization with increased agility and improved collaboration across traditional organizational boundaries should consider how to decouple rigid job structures from the individuals that fill them, and think about using roles (rather than jobs) with people taking on multiple roles to suit the circumstances.

Roles prescribe competencies which people must demonstrate to perform a given function

Roles fit particularly well in the context of Web 2.0 and the shift to the digital enterprise. Processes call out roles needed to execute them. Roles prescribe competencies (knowledge, skills, and behaviors) which people must demonstrate to perform a given function. This works regardless of reporting structure (i.e., who reports to whom), and where an individual is placed on the organizational chart.

Transformational Change

Defining transformational change can be tricky as it is inherently subjective. From the perspective of IT leadership, a change in a business analyst's role (for example from a business area focus to an end-to-end business process focus) may appear to be an incremental change. To the analyst that change might feel transformational.

Notwithstanding this subjectivity, transformational change can be defined as:
- **Broad in scope** (i.e., encompassing change in processes, tools, organization structure, vision, mission, rewards, and recognition)
- **Deep in nature** (i.e., intended to lead to breakthrough in organizational outcomes)
- **Far-reaching in impact** (i.e., affecting a broad base of stakeholders)
- **Recognized to be risky** (i.e., both the absolute details of the end state and the journey will be unclear or ambiguous at the outset)

Not all transformational change is intended. Given the complex nature if IT organiza-

> ## Authentic Promises: An Example
>
> *Imagine a personal trainer saying, "I am going to transform you into a fitter, healthier person who will look better and live longer. Here are your exercises and diet plan." While she might be willing to make that promise, it is false and I am likely to be disappointed and to lose interest quickly.*
>
> *Imagine if, on the other hand, she said, "I'm going to teach you some exercises and show you a diet plan. If you do the exercises as taught and change your eating habits per the diet plan, you will over time transform into a fitter, healthier person who will look better, and live longer." Now that is an authentic promise.*
>
> *The real transformation is to transform me. Can I really get myself to exercise and eat per her recommendations?*

tions, sometimes an intervention that looks on the surface to be purely incremental is subject to the infamous *butterfly effect* that leads to unexpected transformational change.

For similar reasons (i.e., the unpredictable behaviors of complex systems), not all programs intended to be transformational actually result in transformation. In fact, the vast majority do not. Countless transformational programs with titles like *Quality First* or *One Company* or *Journey to Innovation* began with enthusiasm, and are now distant memories with little more to show for them than printed tee shirts and logo mugs.

Principles for Transforming IT Capabilities
Here are three leadership principles that apply to transformational change:

Principle #1. Communicate from the outset with absolute integrity and the unvarnished truth. Tell what you know, speculate when you must, but make clear that it's speculation and be prepared to say, "I don't know but we will jointly figure it out," when you honestly don't know.

IT people are smart and will not be easily fooled. Trying to fool them will undoubtedly backfire. So it is important to engage them in the dialog, to be honest about what is going to be needed, and to avoid taking anything off the table as a sacred cow that is not to be discussed.

In most transformations, some people will not make it through. That is a fact that cannot be hidden or avoided. It is important to make it clear to people that, although there are no guarantees, those who engage in the journey are more likely to come out as winners. On the other hand, those that stand in the background lobbing stones will come out disappointed.

Principle #2. Take the time to collaboratively build a compelling but plausible vision for the future.

The temptation is to short-change this step. IT leaders have a vision in their heads, and they assume everyone else in the organization understands it when, in fact, they don't share the vision. The next temptation is to develop the vision with a subset of the IT leadership team, then emboss it on a paper weight or memorialize it on wall-sized posters. After all the wordsmithing and polishing is complete, the vision statement (which is merely a thin sliver of the vision) means little to anybody except to the select few who created it.

Visions must be rich and multi-faceted. They need to be compelling. They need to serve a higher purpose that gets people up in the morning and excited to go to work.

The Path to IT Transformation

Some years ago I participated in a series of CIO forums across the US sponsored by Microsoft Windows Azure. It was a fascinating experience. Much of the discussion in our panel Q&A was around the challenge of moving legacy systems to the cloud.

While this might be an interesting, cost reduction play, the best cases I have seen use the cloud for things you can't easily do today (such as helping Mary lift sales with a cloud-based CRM as described in the scenario on the following page). That is where I believe the path to IT transformation can begin or, for those who are already on that path, how IT transformation can be accelerated.

Business operations wanted the maximum flexibility implied by the enterprise software package while IT was mostly concerned about control and protecting the users from doing something in the name of configuration that might damage the system or data integrity.

My suggestion was an intervention where we would move beyond territorial issues to collaboratively build the process that would be used to manage configuration changes. The process would point to roles that, in turn, would identify competencies needed to fill given roles.

They need to be in people's heads, hearts, and stomachs, and they must justify putting staff through the pain, anxiety, and risks of change.

Sometimes it is better to plan on a quiet start and a loud finish rather than the other way around. After all, a transformation is an outcome more than it is a plan or intent. Rather than promise an IT transformation, the focus should be on what the IT team is going to change, what the team is going to do differently, what new outcomes will

Convergence of Business and Consumer IT

The convergence of business and consumer IT is having a dramatic impact on corporate IT. Imagine the following scenario.

Mary, a sales and marketing vice president, approaches her IT organization with a request to implement a CRM solution. "Yes, we can do that. It will take about 2 years to do and it will cost about $20 Million, give or take 30%, but we can't get to it until next year." Mary then sees an ad for CRM in the cloud and calls the vendor.

The vendor says, "Yes, we can get you started today. It's probably best to start with a pilot group which we can do for $40 per user per month. We can then bring the cost per user down as you scale up the number of users. Plus you get a 30-day free trial to make sure our solution fits your needs."

So what should Mary do? She's been charged with driving up sales and she's convinced that a CRM solution is a key tool to do so. Easy choice, right? She goes ahead with the cloud solution. Variations on this scenario are playing out every day.

Now imagine that when Mary comes to IT, the BRM provides the answer first before Mary reaches out to a vendor. "Yes, Mary, we can help you deploy a CRM solution. We've been investigating cloud solutions for this type of need and there are very attractive options. We can get you started almost immediately and without massive capital outlays."

Even better, imagine that the BRM approached Mary before she approached IT and told her about the potential for a low-cost way to boost sales with a CRM capability.

More visionary IT leaders are encouraging their BRM teams to partner with the Mary's in their companies. BRMs are helping the business choose the right vendor and deal with issues such as privacy, security, and data ownership. Less visionary leaders are in denial, believing that IT belongs in IT, and the cloud is a passing fad.

Mary is going ahead with the cloud solution anyway. The only question is, does she do it behind corporate IT's back, or with their blessing, help, and guidance?

result, and why those outcomes are valid and worthwhile.

Principle #3. IT can't be transformed by transforming IT

The performance of the IT organization (except for basic IT infrastructure services) is the product of Business-IT performance. It is ultimately the way that businesses harness the potential value of the IT organization that is being transformed, rather than the IT organization that is the subject of transformation. There is little value in the IT organization introducing a new investment prioritization process designed to shift IT investments to a more innovation-focused profile if this is not embraced by business leaders.

The Convergence of Consumer IT and Business IT

IT is becoming ever more central to what an enterprise does and how it does it. IT for consumers (e.g., iPhones, iPads, Kindles, Facebook, eBay), and IT for business are converging. Business people are consumers. Their customers are consumers.

How people navigate their personal lives spills over into their business lives, and vice versa. New workers join the workforce with an unprecedented IT literacy and a set of expectations about how they will work, collaborate, and communicate.

Consumer devices and services not only allow people to work in different ways (mobile, for example), they also allow individuals to do different types of work. An example of this is *sentiment analysis*.
- What are customers, prospects, and competitors saying about the company?
- What are they saying about location-based services?
- Are they participating in communities of interest or practice?

The Need for IT Renewal

Progressive IT leaders will reposition the IT organization as a business enabler no matter how and where IT capabilities are sourced.

> *Progressive IT leaders will reposition the IT organization as a business enabler no matter how and where IT capabilities are sourced*

In many respects, core IT roles are shifting towards Business Relationship Manager, enterprise architect, and integrator rather than manager of data centers and server farms, developer of systems, and manager of projects. This shift can be understood as IT transformation.

The Cloud is Both a Driver and an Enabler of IT Transformation

The key roles of an IT organization are being changed by the inevitable emergence of the cloud as an option in the delivery of IT services. IT organizations also leverage the cloud to enable and drive IT transformation.

This section describes three major opportunities for cloud computing to accelerate IT transformation:

1. Finding and validating new business opportunities
2. Improving existing business capabilities
3. Transforming how IT capabilities are managed and deployed

Finding and Validating New Business Opportunities

Cloud-based services make it relatively easy for a business to experiment with new products, services, and even new business models. Not having to procure or build costly infrastructure can reduce, or even eliminate, capital outlay. It can speed time to market, and ensure future flexibility as market conditions and competitive responses change.

Short lead times, the ability to better align costs with benefits, and the flexibility to scale up or down as needed, represent attractive value propositions for those wanting to explore the unknown.

An added attraction for using the cloud to explore new business opportunities is that the need to integrate with existing systems and data is typically less than that associated with replacing or upgrading existing solutions.

Improving Business Capabilities

Due to the need for interfaces to existing systems, improving business capabilities with cloud-based services can be more challenging than renewing the IT organization as described above. It can still represent a worthwhile approach, especially if current capabilities are lacking.

Improving business capabilities with cloud-based services can be more challenging than renewing the IT organization

For those who have been diligent about service oriented architecture, interfacing legacy applications with cloud services should not present a significant challenge. For those who have been proactive around business analytics and data warehousing, building necessary data interfaces should not be a concern.

Transforming How IT Capabilities are Managed and Deployed

This is a particularly exciting cloud-driven change for several reasons:

- Traditionally IT organizations are quite basic in their own use of IT. They often manage IT capabilities and assets via Excel spreadsheets, email, and lots and lots of meetings.
- Moving to the cloud is inevitable. The only question for CIOs and the IT professionals that report to them is: *will we lead the shift or be left in the dark while our business clients and customers race to the cloud?* Leveraging the cloud for internal IT purposes is one way of getting ahead of the game, at least in terms of learning and experience.
- The nature of IT work, with its complexity and knowledge intensiveness, lends itself to a more collaborative and networked approach which, in turn, lends itself to a cloud-based platform.

Leveraging Cloud Services for Internal Use

As business and IT converge, the management of IT assets and capabilities is becoming more complex, more distributed, and more collaborative. This challenges IT organizations to find effective ways to leverage cloud services for internal use.

IT Management as a Distributed Activity

Roles that were traditionally held by IT professionals (such as business analytics and application configuration) are migrating into the business units. At the same time, IT professionals are assuming new roles such as sourcing managers, information brokers, and enterprise architects.

Software as a Service (SaaS) and IT Transformation

The SaaS movement is spreading quickly and is already a sourcing strategy worthy of consideration. I have no doubt that it will become a dominant form of sourcing. SaaS strategies should be considered in conjunction with service oriented architecture (SOA) strategies.

I believe that SaaS, viewed in the context of SOA, is one of many new sourcing strategies and that much of the future software and its sub-components that run our companies and agencies will be pulled from the ether. We will care far more about business functionality and results, and less about who wrote it and where it runs.

I acknowledge that there are still many issues to be worked out, and valid questions about security, privacy, and vendor business models to resolve, but I believe these will be worked out satisfactorily over the next few years.

Five Cs in the Cloud: An Example

I worked with a client who was refining their IT operating model to enable a new, growth-oriented Business-IT strategy. They had determined that they wanted to support their IT work and forge stronger business relationships using Microsoft Share-Point.

They were on SharePoint 2007 and recognized that they needed to move to SharePoint 2010 as their preferred collaboration and knowledge management platform. The upgrades to servers, licenses and related IT infrastructure was going to take 3-4 months and represented a significant capital outlay. At the same time, they did not want to lose the momentum they had already established in developing the new Business-IT strategy.

As an alternative, we were able to set them up with a cloud-hosted SharePoint instance over one weekend with zero capital outlay and a very modest monthly cost that scales with the number of users and, therefore, with value delivered.

Now they are creating new levels of organizational clarity, establishing a continuously improving IT operating model, and experiencing new ways of collaborating, coordinating, connecting, co-creating and coalescing through a set of cloud-based software services.

IT Management as a Complex Activity

As IT management expands beyond the traditional roles of the IT professional to the emerging roles of information *prosumers*, the complexity of IT environments is increasing. There are many ways IT can turn the increasing complexity of the IT environment to its advantage.

The study of complex systems offers important insights on this subject. It teaches that organization is a natural, spontaneous act, and that emergent structures are more resilient than imposed hierarchy and control. It reveals that creativity arises from variety and randomness. It highlights the importance of relationships, porous boundaries, free flows of information, and self-reference.

The Five Cs of Information Management

As the management of IT becomes increasingly distributed and complex, five types of management activity emerge as important to the ways work is done. These *five Cs of information management* are ideally suited to cloud-based services.

1. Collaborating

2. Coordinating
3. Connecting
4. Co-creating
5. Coalescing

Enabling the Five Cs in the Cloud

Because each of these activities is increasingly being conducted across time and space, and across organizational boundaries, enabling them through flexible, scalable cloud solutions becomes an attractive proposition. The following sub-sections take each topic in turn, and explore how they can help organizations manage IT in the cloud.

Collaborating on IT Work

Much IT work is performed through teams that are increasingly distributed across geographies, organizations and time zones. This change forces a shift in work management from a document-centric (write-attach-email-review-attach-email, repeat ad infinitum) to a more collaborative Wiki-based approach.

In this environment, a Wiki approach has significant advantages:
- Wikis are inherently non-linear, and encourage a constructive informality that improves quality over time, drives organizational clarity, and reduces or eliminates redundancy and contradictions. Well-managed Wikis let participants stop wondering which document is the most current version, and what has changed since the

Is The Federated IT Operating Model Doomed?

Today most organizations employ some sort of federated IT operating model. Wikipedia defines a federation as characterized by a union of partially self-governing states or regions united by a central (federal) government.

Typically under this model, enterprise-wide or common applications, initiatives and infrastructure are a centralized (federal) responsibility, while local applications and activities are under the control of business units or functions. This federal rights/ states rights model has infinite variations.

Just as in countries with a federal governance model, competing forces between state and federal rights pull and push over time, leading to an ebb and flow of centralization and decentralization. It is never static. It constantly responds to the forces of change, just as all living systems breathe in some way or another and have their seasonal variations. Every now and again, new forces surface and combine to disrupt the gentle ebb and flow. The American Civil War comes to mind.

last version.
- Wikis encourage multi-author collaboration. The typical document-centric approach has one or two main authors with everyone else in a review role. Wikis encourage a more collaborative approach to authoring with higher engagement and understanding in the content.
- A Wiki approach dramatically simplifies search and discovery. The ability to hyperlink, tag and use a well-factored semantic Wiki leads to content that is far more accessible, intelligible, and searchable for all stakeholders.
- The BRM Institute Members Online Campus, built on a Confluence Wiki, houses the highly structured BRM Interactive Body of Knowledge and dozens of interest groups, communities of practice, member hangouts and more, all operating as a collaborative resource that has passed the test of time with over 5 years experience by thousands of members.

Coordinating Activities in Time and Space
As IT work becomes more distributed, the need to coordinate activities in time and space becomes increasingly important and challenging. SaaS offerings are ideally suited to helping distributed teams coordinate their activities through:
- Real-time communication and collaboration
- Collaborative project management
- Desktop video conferencing

Connecting People and Ideas
The need to identify and connect people and ideas is important to innovation and learning. As IT work becomes more distributed, cloud-based SaaS solutions become effective ways of connecting people and ideas through tools such as:

As IT work becomes more distributed, cloud-based SaaS solutions become effective ways of connecting people and ideas

- Social networking
- Mind mapping
- Virtual electronic white boards
- Social network analysis
- Innovation jams

Co-creating Experiences
As business and IT converge, opportunities emerge to co-create experiences with customers, consumers, suppliers, and business partners. New types of SaaS solutions for co-creation include:
- Modeling and simulation

- Prototyping
- Virtual worlds

Coalescing Around Ideas and Reaching Consensus on Decisions
With increasing distribution of IT work comes the need to poll stakeholders, tap into sentiment, coalesce around ideas, and reach consensus around decisions. New ap-

---

IT Transformation: Real or Reorganization?

One of the great things about being a consultant is that I get to see recurring patterns. One of the sad things about being a consultant is seeing the same mistakes being made over and over, sometimes in the same organization. Over the years I've been involved in literally dozens of IT transformations. This is how the conversation with a potential new client often goes (leaving out many sordid steps):

Client: "We are planning an IT transformation. Can you help us?"

VM: "Yes. I avoid the term transformation. I prefer to think in terms of transition. This is more palatable, and in terms of an IT operating model, gets to all the moving parts you have to consider such as services, capabilities, competencies, behaviors, rules of engagement, mission-identity-vision, metrics, sourcing, governance and organization structure. It also recognizes that transition is continuous and never finished."

Client: "That sounds great! When can you start?"

At the engagement kick-off the client will show me the current organization chart and a couple of variations of the new organization chart. Their expectation is that we are going to work through the pros and cons of alternate organizational structures, choose the best one, and begin what they think of as IT transformation.

The Good News
If they are fortunate, they have engaged someone who:
- *Has a boatload of experience in both successful and failed IT transformations.*
- *Has enough gray hairs, money in the bank, an instinct to preserve his sanity and is more than happy to tell the client they are going down a desperately wrong path, show them why and refuse to be part of it.*

The Bad News
If they are less fortunate they:
- *Have engaged someone who will do whatever they ask while nodding wisely and making soothing noises.*
- *Or they go it alone. After all, who needs a consultant to reorganize?*

proaches and supporting tools emerging in this space include:
- Polling
- Group decision making
- Prediction markets

The New Forces of Change

IT governance is undergoing a confluence of new forces including:

- **Cloud computing.** It is easier, faster, and cheaper (on the face of it) to leverage the cloud to host applications, and provide IT services (e.g., storage, transaction processing, data analytics) rather than to have a federal IT group provide these services. Much of this activity takes place in the realm of shadow IT.

- **Mobile computing.** More people are doing more via smart phones and tablets. This exposes consumers to mobile applications and the many app stores including Apple and Google. Getting an app is as simple as clicking a button, and many apps are free or cheap enough to add to a mobile phone bill without feeling any pain.

- **The shift in the personal computing operating system**, from Windows—which can be controlled by the central (federal) IT department—to technologies such as Apple's iOS and Google's Android which are much harder (perhaps impossible) to control centrally.

- **Browser-based applications.** SaaS is easy now because everyone is targeting basically the same UI platform—the W3C compliant browser. This is making apps universal in their look and feel, and standards like Bootstrap make device independence a relatively easy task.

- **Application Integrators.** REST APIs, tools like Zapier, SSO standards like SAML and OpenID Connect completely change the landscape of integrating apps from barriers to enablers.

Rearranging the Deck Chairs On The Titanic

Reorganization driven by changing the organization chart is often described as rearranging the deck chairs on a sinking ship. In reality it's worse than that. Reorganizations generally:

1. *Break things that were working fine*
2. *Throw people into panic and confusion*
3. *Don't lead to any positive behavior change*
4. *Disrupt work flows that, even if inefficient, at least work*
5. *Consume lots of time and emotional energy*
6. *Force people to focus internally while their business partners see a dysfunctional and unresponsive IT organization get even worse*

7-Steps to a Mutually Adjusting IT Operating Model

Responding to Change

The genie is out of the bottle and it is not going back any time soon. Change is inevitable. How IT organizations respond to change is optional. Here are three possibilities:

1. **Take a laissez-faire approach**. This is the path of least resistance.
2. **Push back, hunker down, and reinforce the federal model** with more controls and stronger sanctions for shadow behavior.
3. **Adopt a mutual adjustment approach** that navigates the stormy waters to constantly find the optimal balance.

History shows that options 1 and 2 have a potential for creating unintended consequences. For example, many central IT groups—choosing option 1—were slow to respond to the emergence of the personal computer. When they did respond, it was generally following option 2. They tried to constrain the use of PCs which, in turn, resulted in rogue and shadow behavior that set IT efforts back several years in many companies.

In most situations, option 3 is the pragmatic solution. Some form of central coordination of infrastructure is needed, and many unknowns will emerge to shape how forces will play out over time. There is no right or wrong answer here.

There is only a critical need for organizational clarity so that the bounds of infrastructure are set clearly, and set in a way that is appropriate to the times, and to the business context. At the same time, there is a need to address the inevitable influence of the shadow IT phenomenon that allows much IT activity to happen outside the realm of IT governance.

> *The definition of terms are subject to interpretation and tend to change over time*

The meaning of terms like *central coordination*, *enterprise-wide* and *infrastructure* must be clearly defined, then re-defined from time to time as the industry gains experience with cloud computing and consumerization of IT. These definitions are subject to interpretation and tend to change over time, with changes in business conditions, leadership, technology, and other forces.

Seven Steps to a Mutually Adjusting IT Operating Model

IT leaders must approach modifications to the IT operating model in the same way they would approach any needed change:

1. Create and market a compelling end state vision.
2. Surface and sell the cost of status quo or of going down the wrong path.
3. Define a credible and palatable path to the future.
4. Enroll key stakeholders in joining together on that path.
5. Engage selected key stakeholders in the governance model.
6. Surface and celebrate successes along the way.
7. Take action to discourage deviations from the path.

This 7-step process helps IT leaders recognize organizational dysfunctions, and gain insights into the default future for their organizations.

IT Operating Model Transition 101

The correct approach (with many variations on this theme) goes something like this:

A. Define the IT Operating Model

1. Agree to the IT organization's mission and the reason for its existence.
2. Agree to the vision the IT organization wants to be, and the identity by which it wants to be known.
3. Define IT services as they are viewed by business partners (the view from outside IT, not from within).
4. Define needed capabilities to deliver those services.

5. Define processes needed by those capabilities.
6. Define needed roles and technologies to execute those processes.
7. Define competencies needed to fill those roles and manage those technologies.
8. Define how to source capabilities, competencies and technologies.
9. Define the Business-IT governance model and how decisions will be made and enforced.
10. Define the optimal grouping of resources and linking mechanisms among resource groupings (i.e., the organization structure itself).

B. Define the Transition Approach
1. Define the major transition work streams.
2. Build the transition and organizational change plan.
3. Appoint an overall transition program manager.
4. Appoint transition work stream leads.
5. Create a compelling and clearly communicated case for transition including why transition is necessary, how transition will address performance gaps and challenges, and how people will be engaged in transition.

C. Launch the Transition
1. If this all sounds like a lot of work, it is.

The Big Lessons
1. Reorganizations do more harm than good, and rarely deliver any positive change.
2. Transition to a more effective IT operating model is hard work, and fraught with human challenges.
3. Don't undertake a transition unless there is a strong case for change, a clear sense of how the transition will solve problems, and a determination to communicate over and over until everyone gets it and is engaged in the transition.
4. When working through the IT operating model questions, two things become apparent. The organization structure literally falls out naturally at the end of the IT operating model analysis, and the importance of the organization structure becomes significantly reduced.

Collaborative Change: Finding Order In Chaos 8

People don't resist change. They resist being changed.

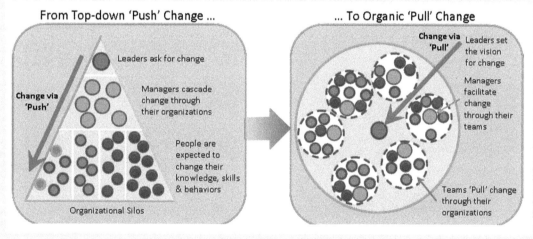

Organizational Change as an Organic Process

Can you really manage change as if it were a project to be delivered? Are traditional methods of organizational change flawed?

Overview

This Chapter addresses the thorny subject of organizational change, particularly with complex, far reaching change such as the culture change associated with transforming an IT operating model. It looks at ways to approach organizational change and the importance of momentum in leading change. Finally, it introduces contemporary collaborative approaches to change that are appropriate to enabling a digital enterprise.

Collaborative Change: Finding Order In Chaos

Change Management or Change Leadership?

The term *organizational change management* is a misnomer. Change can't be managed in the ways that people and projects can. It can be inspired. It can be led. It can be facilitated. It can be subverted and rejected. But it can't be managed with any certainty as to outcomes.

Change leadership is a more appropriate term, and everyone in an organization should be a leader of the change they would like to see. When a change is suggested that a team or individual knows is not needed, or would prefer not to happen, then it becomes the responsibility of change advocates to lead others into the light, and to persuade the nay-sayers to get on-board with the change. Either approach is a leadership issue.

So Much Known, So Little Applied

There is a substantial body of research and theory about organizational change management (OCM) dating back to the mid-50s and earlier. Over the decades, countless first-hand experiences have been documented about the process of changing personal behavior and the behavior of colleagues, friends, and family members, accompanied by recommendations for success. Books on change date back to the early 1940s, and a current search on Amazon.com yields 11,860 titles.

In spite of all the books about, and methodologies for, organizational change that have been published, studies indicate the results of organizational change management initiatives remain disappointing. Most findings on OCM seem to resonate with people who are facing, or who have faced, organizational change.

That so many change initiatives fail to meet their objectives would suggest that nearly all of the findings and recommendations from the body of OCM knowledge are woefully lacking in information that actually increases the success rate of organizational change management initiatives.

The irony is that with so much known about organizational change, most organizations are inept at making significant change happen. Clearly, for all the apparent wisdom, the discipline is fraught with subtleties and complexities.

IT Professionals and Organizational Change

Organizational change in IT organizations is particularly problematic. Few IT professionals are adept at organizational change. This is a sweeping generalization, of course, but one that has been shown to be true by numerous studies conducted by industry analysts over many years.

A possible reason for this may be the characteristics of the IT profession that draw people to it. Whether due to nature or nurture, IT professionals:

- Are oriented to tangible, finite projects, and deliverables
- Like plans with beginnings, middles and ends, defined deliverables, and clear milestones
- Take on highly ambiguous problems that must ultimately be reduced to simple, non-ambiguous solutions

Organizational change has none of these characteristics. It is about people, politics, and influence, not routines, components,and processes. It is about learning, not just

---

Organizational Change Management or Change Management
For IT professionals, even the terminology can be confusing.

I had a long and, I thought, enlightening conversation with a CIO some years back about the challenges and importance of managing change. I was talking about the soft stuff (which is so hard) of organizational change management.

About an hour into the conversation, it became apparent that he was talking about technical change management—configuration management, release control, testing, and release management.

Once the communication disconnect had surfaced, the CIO revealed that he had never heard of organizational change management as a discipline.

> ## Challenge of Change: A Personal Experience
> *In my very first blog post in 2007, I mentioned my trepidation at entering the blogosphere. (What I am calling trepidation others might refer to as resistance to change.)*
>
> *In 2007, when it was suggested to me by my boss that I should write a blog, my first reaction was: I don't have the time or skills. This translated to an ability issue. My second reaction was: I'm afraid of making a fool of myself. This translated to a willingness issue.*
>
> *Left at that, I'd still be thinking about blogging (or not) rather than learning my way through it.*
>
> *Is change resistance real, normal, inevitable? How does it play out in climbing the IT maturity and value curve? Two lessons can be learned from my blogging experience.*
>
> *First, people tend to hold onto the status quo because, good or bad, like it or not, it is predictable. As human beings, we (mostly) seek out predictability. Second, our tendency to hold on to the status quo can become a significant force when the changes we are expected to make either:*
> - *Require new abilities we might not have (or might not know we have)*
> - *Require a willingness to involve ourselves in the change and its associated risks*

doing. Leading or participating in organizational change means living with ambiguity, and IT folks don't like ambiguity.

For all the change that IT organizations bring about for their business partners, IT people are generally resistant to change. This resistance is deeply rooted in several factors:

1. IT environments are full of technical complexity. They contain layers upon layers of technology which, in turn, contain multitudes of interfaces and dependencies. Change something over here and something over there is impacted—sometimes in subtle ways that may not be evident for some time, or until some other seemingly unrelated change is made.
2. IT professionals thrive by taking complex situations and reducing them down to binary zeroes and ones.
3. There is no room for ambiguity in a digital system. For this reason, IT specialists are conditioned to abhor ambiguity.

In contrast, change is full of ambiguity. What has been in the past is no longer, and what will be in the future is not yet stabilized. The natural inclination of IT professionals, then, is to drive out the ambiguity. Typically, the fastest, safest path to predictability is to end the change initiative before damage is done, or before the changed state is reached, and to revert to the status quo.

Resistance to Change: An Example

It's a familiar adage that if you are trying to persuade people to embrace or engage in change, you need to get to the heart of the what's in it for me (WIFM) factor. I've been helping clients understand, embrace and lead change initiatives for about forty years.

More and more frequently, I am personally on the receiving end of a change. I learned many years ago that being trained and certified in change management does not immunize me from the stresses of change.

A personal change experience is quite telling of how I (and probably others) react to those stresses. Some years ago, I found myself in a discussion with colleagues about web browsers in general, and Mozilla Firefox in particular. I am no laggard when it comes to technology adoption, but I'm no early adopter either. I won't lightly embark on a change unless I can:

- *See a very compelling benefit to the change*
- *Understand and be comfortable with the risks of change (compared with the risks of not changing)*
- *Understand the path I'm going to take from current state to changed state (in this case, learning a new browser technology, moving all my favorite links, etc.)*

I'm pretty conservative with my work technologies. Internet Explorer (IE) came with my laptop computer and seemed to be adequate for my needs. I asked my colleagues, who were all enthusiastic about Firefox, why I should change to Firefox. I heard a lot of noise. They told me about features that I did not understand, could not visualize, or simply did not interest me. They sent me links to evaluation sites. I spent a few minutes on those but, once again, I could not see anything compelling that would lead me to undertake the risks of change. After a few conversations, I dropped the idea of switching browsers and continued with the more familiar IE.

Then I came across a comment about Firefox's speed advantage over IE. Now I was really interested! In my value system as it relates to personal computing, I'm a speed freak! I crave fast response times. When I learned that Firefox might be faster than IE, I took the plunge and installed Firefox. If my colleagues had known, or had flushed out, my personal value system, and had they associated the browser change to my need for speed, instead of throwing features and benefits at me to which I could not relate, I would have jumped at the browser change when it was first suggested without hesitation.

Another reason for change resistance in IT organizations is that organizational change requires energy. Rarely, however, do IT managers budget the extra time and resources needed for the change. People are expected to do their normal workload, plus assimilate change. This is a recipe for frustration and failure.

Overcoming the Challenge of Change: A Personal Experience

So what mitigated my ability and willingness issues with blogging described in the story on page 165? First, as a by-product of the acquisition of The Concours Group (my employer) by BSG Alliance, I became exposed to a new vision and ambition for our firm. Our new CEO clearly believed that if we are going to help our clients on their journeys to becoming digital enterprises, we must first become a digital enterprise. The message was important.

The fact that he modeled appropriate behaviors, including the rapid deployment of a company-wide social network and collaboration hub, took us beyond mere rhetoric into something real and tangible. As a by-product of this collaboration activity, I quickly got exposed to new terms, trends and technologies. My eyes were opened!

At the same time, one of my colleagues—Susan Scrupski, a highly regarded and influential blogger—reached out to me and offered to be my blog coach. She effectively held my hand, pointed me at things to read, tools to try, and guidelines to follow.

All of this made it relatively safe to get on the web and try some stuff with her watching from afar to keep me on track or tell me when and how to get back on track. In this way, my ability issues were addressed through a relatively simple collaboration with someone who was a master blogger!

What of my willingness issues? It quickly became apparent that blogging provided potential value to our colleagues and clients. It also became apparent that I would learn through blogging—a point that was not intuitively obvious but was one of the insights I gained from Susan. Last, but not least, it became apparent that blogging behavior was valued by our firm leadership. As my ability issues were addressed, so were my willingness issues.

To net this out, a clear vision of why blogging was important to our firm was effectively and passionately communicated by our CEO. That vision went beyond mere rhetoric by specific actions that supported and made tangible that vision. In support of the vision, expectations for me about ways I could participate in realizing the vision were communicated (and modeled) by several key opinion leaders in the firm. Finally, I was assigned a coach and change agent to ease me in to the blogosphere and help me overcome my ability and willingness deficits.

Another challenge for IT teams is the term *organizational change management*. The terminology is confusing at best, and misleading at worse, because it is too close to *change management*—the technical function associated with ensuring that changes to a system are implemented with high integrity.

For this reason, when creating the BRM Institute knowledge base and training, we adopted Business Transition Management as an alternative to organizational change management.

From Push Change Leadership

Traditional organizational change methods are generally based on a push model of change. We (company leadership) want you (employees) to work differently (e.g., reengineered processes, new incentive/reward systems, new tools/technologies, new organization structures, mergers/de-mergers, and so on). There is something inherently manipulative about this approach and reminiscent of Taylor's philosophy: leaders are smart and know what to do; workers are dumb and must be told what to do. (For additional information on Taylor, see p. 182.)

I believe that the types of changes many companies are attempting to engage in today require that both hearts and minds be engaged in the change. It's not enough for employees simply to follow a new process. They must truly understand and wholeheartedly embrace the values and ideals behind the process. They must want to follow the new process (or whatever the change being implemented is), not do so just because they've been told to. Ensuring an exceptional customer experience, for example, does not simply happen because your customer-facing employees follow new procedures.

Change that requires engagement of hearts and minds is far more likely to take hold with a pull approach. I'd argue that most of the changes around Enterprise 2.0 very much lend themselves to a pull approach, or at least to more of a balance between push and pull change models.

To Pull Change Leadership

Becoming a digital enterprise requires more of a pull approach to organizational change management, and the good news is that Web 2.0 lends itself to enabling this kind of change. Of course there's a catch 22 here. If people aren't using Web 2.0 or, as in some companies, they are not allowed to use it, then these tools can't be leveraged to facilitate change.

A comparison between push and pull leadership styles is shown in the graphic at the beginning of this Chapter (p. 161)

Changing or Being Changed

The common assertion that people hate change is a misconception or, at least a misstatement. People make changes all the time. For every person that has a cautious, conservative approach to change, there are others that embrace, and even seek out change.

A Rule of Thumb for Change

One rule of thumb for change is that when change is introduced, one-third will be highly receptive to the change and will make the change without being prodded. One-third will be highly resistant to the change and will fight it tooth and nail. And one-third will look to the other two-thirds before deciding which path to follow. This may be overly simplistic, but the hypothesis resonates because it matches the experience of many change leaders.

> *People don't hate change. They hate being changed*

People don't hate change. They hate being changed. This is a key distinction. Successful change engages the people who must change in the change, and makes clear to them why change is beneficial to them (*what's in it for me*).

When presented in this way, people will flock to change. Or at least one third of them will. One third will fight it all the way, while the middle third will watch to see how the metaphorical wind is blowing before committing to one side or the other.

Different Types of Change

Change is a complex and multi-faceted concept, so any generalizations about it are fraught with problems. Changing a simple routine (for example, a new way for employees to record time) is quite different from moving to a new boss.

Changing a routine is relatively simple. A more extreme form of change is culture change. To become customer focused—as some change programs proclaim—is significantly easier to say than to make reality. Culture change requires leadership and employees to:
- Understand what behavior changes are expected
- Believe in the need for those changes
- Develop required knowledge, skills, and behaviors
- Be willing to invest significant effort, and take personal risk to make required changes

Organizational Change Leadership: From Push to Pull

Organizational change planning should be based upon more pull and less push (as shown in the graphic at the beginning of this Chapter (p. 161)), and continuously revised in light of emergent behaviors. Sometimes emergent behaviors actually precede the recognition of the need for change.

For example, many IT organizations today are trying (and often failing) to leverage social networking. At the same time, members of the IT organization are participating in social networks both within their companies, and with external communities (e.g., Facebook, LinkedIn). So while IT leaders are trying to manage a social network initiative, the reality is that social networking is already happening, but in an unplanned and emergent way.

If planned efforts can surface and leverage emergent activities, there is a better chance that social networking can be steered towards improved outcomes for the IT community and for the company.

Techniques such as Appreciative Inquiry may be useful:
- Find out where the desired change has already happened in the organization
- Determine the conditions that led to the success
- Figure out how to replicate the conditions that led to success

The future is already here. It is just not evenly distributed

As author William Gibson has suggested, the future is already here. It is just not evenly distributed.

The Importance of Consequences
When there is a lack of consequences for working with, rather than against, a change program, many people will instinctively return to their old way of doing things. If there are no positive consequences for those who embrace change, and/or no negative consequences for those who reject it, then the middle third will likely reject the change. The critical mass will never materialize, and the change is a lost cause.

Taking Care of Organizational Change Management
Today, most large management consulting firms offer services from their OCM practices, and some world-class companies continue to foster and practice OCM disciplines. There are also a number of boutique consulting firms that specialize in this discipline. But in the general population of enterprises around the world, OCM expertise is sorely lacking, and the evidence of failed, painful, or disappointing change experiences is commonplace.

Mechanistic and Emergent Change Models

Harvard Business School Professor John Kotter researched and wrote extensively on organizational change and proposed an 8-step change model ("Why Transformation Efforts Fail", Harvard Business Review (1995). The Kotter model implies linearity and assumes predictability and manageability of the change processes. John Kotter's change process suggests we should:

1. *Establish a sense of urgency*
2. *Create a guiding coalition*
3. *Develop a vision and strategy*
4. *Communicate the change vision*
5. *Empower broad based action*
6. *Generate short term wins*
7. *Consolidate gains and produce more change*
8. *Anchor change in the new culture*

In the last 20 years, a more organic and emergent view of organizational change has surfaced—one that leverages chaos and complexity theory. For example, Wanda J. Orlikowski and J. Debra Hofman, "An Improvisational Model of Change Management: The Case of Groupware Technologies" (1995) and C. L. White, Change On Demand: The Science of Turbo Charging Change in Millennium Corporations *(2012).*

Emergent models for organizational change should not been seen as alternatives to more mechanistic models (such as Kotter's). Rather they should be treated as refinements that help to interpret and apply mechanistic models.

How to Manage Without Organizational Change Expertise

For the most significant change programs (for example, implementing an enterprise-wide resource planning suite), companies typically engage one of the major management consulting firms or specialty boutique firms that bring their OCM experts and methodologies. The rest muddle along, mostly oblivious to the OCM discipline, gradually coming to the realization that their major cultural change initiatives will fall short of their needs and expectations.

While there are many times when deep OCM expertise is essential and it makes sense to bring in OCM consultants, there are other times when it is not feasible to bring in outside gurus, and local organizational change expertise is warranted.

Project and program data suggest that smaller projects experience better success rates than do large ones. But even small projects are subject to value leakage, and create

> ### Change Agent: The Missing Ingredient in Organizational Change
>
> *I've worked with many companies who were trying to improve business performance by implementing business process change enabled by IT. I've also worked with IT organizations who were trying to improve their performance by deploying an IT strategy or by transforming their IT operating model. It was always a frustrating process, usually painful, and often yielding disappointing results.*
>
> *Some 40 years ago, I discovered the missing ingredient. A fortuitous meeting with organizational change guru Daryl Conner enlightened me to the fact that there was a discipline called organizational change management (OCM)—one that could be learned and supported by a toolkit. I learned about the role of change agent, which can be a focal point for bringing the OCM discipline to bear.*
>
> *Mystery solved. I went through OCM training, began practicing the discipline, and discovered that a formal, well-informed approach to managing organizational change can indeed work to make the difference between success and failure (or at least, accelerate success and grease the skids, as it were).*
>
> *Around the time that my small research and consulting company was acquired by Ernst & Young (E&Y) in 1990. E&Y was establishing an OCM practice by licensing Daryl Conner's training and tools. Around the same time, all the major management consulting firms were establishing some form of OCM practice (most of them by licensing Daryl's intellectual property (IP)). Meanwhile, some companies were establishing their own internal OCM practice (again often based on Daryl's IP). Some, such as General Electric, with their Change Acceleration Process, took the discipline and related toolkit to heart and baked it into their management and leadership training.*
>
> *In BRM Institute's Business Relationship Management training and certification courses, we teach an introduction to this discipline, which we refer to as business transition management. For many corporate clients attending this training, this module is a huge eye-opener! A frequent reaction when client executives are exposed to this material is: "Wow! This is what we've been missing all these years!"*

more stress and confusion than is desirable. That is why small projects can benefit as much from OCM expertise as large projects and programs do. In these situations, where retaining outside resources is not an option, the leadership challenge is to identify where OCM resources should come from. There are two choices:

1. Establish an internal OCM practice.
2. Find an existing role whose mission is concerned with business value realization,

and ensure people in that role are qualified to assist with change management.

Both choices are viable. However, when option 2 is the natural choice, the Business Relationship Manager (if the role exists) is perfect to take on OCM.

The Six-Month Rule of Organizational Change: It's All Personal

It is said that all politics is local. The analogy is that all change is personal. Ultimately, to effect change—such as that involved in introducing a new work process or new tool, increasing collaboration across silos, or improving team effectiveness—individuals must leave behind habits and behaviors ingrained over many years, and adopt new ones.

When trying to persuade people to change, one of the keys is to leverage the WIFM (*what's in it for me*) factor. Helping people understand what's in it for them requires understanding their personal value systems—what are they looking for and what excites them—then determining how the proposed changes can be matched to their value system.

The Six-Month Rule And Why Changes Fail

Anecdotal evidence coupled with experience indicates that it takes at least six months for relatively simple changes in behaviors to become habit. This leads to a *Six-Month Rule* for behavior change. The *Six-Month Rule* applies to changing the behavior demanded of someone who believes in that change.

> *With business attention spans getting ever shorter, an organizational change that will take at least six months to shift behaviors can't be expected to gain traction*

With business attention spans getting ever shorter, an organizational change that will take at least six months to shift behaviors can't be expected to gain traction.

By the time changes begin to take hold, top management has moved on to the next big challenge or opportunity. For this reason a *this too shall pass* response to dictated change is common.

Most of what employees do during a day's work is based on deeply ingrained habit. It is not necessarily the best way, or even the right way, but it is the way that is familiar to them. Most importantly, it is predictable and has predictable results, even if those results are disappointing.

These deeply ingrained behaviors are hard to change, and often derail organizational change initiatives because people balk when they are asked to make behavior chang-

Speed vs. Momentum in Organizational Change

How you pace your major change initiatives is a key factor in achieving organizational change that sticks.

I was teaching an IT leadership development program with a team of senior IT executives, virtually all of them engineers by training and by inclination. It was a very energizing and productive session, loaded with thoughtful dialog and rich, provocative discussion. At one point, while talking about lessons learned in organizational change, one of my colleagues on the faculty stated, "Speed matters. If you don't move fast, the change you are trying to achieve will likely dissipate."

The group's CIO said politely, "No, I think you are confusing speed with momentum. And it is momentum that matters most in organizational change!" This led to an interesting discussion where we rapidly concluded that the CIO was correct. In the process of that discussion, we got a little clearer on the nature of transformational change and some of the critical success factors.

I believe there can be some important insights from this discussion on speed and momentum. We have to sort out some distinctions between the lazy ways we use these terms in everyday speech and their mechanical differences. We tend to use speed and velocity interchangeably. In fact, velocity is a vector—it has direction. Speed is the magnitude of velocity—it doesn't have direction. Strictly speaking, we should be talking about the velocity of change, given that direction is important. You can imagine a situation where I say, "Fred and Anne are both changing their facilitation behaviors very quickly." We might think that's a good thing, but if Fred is becoming a more effective facilitator, while Anne is becoming less effective, that's not a good thing.

The speed/velocity distinction is important to understanding momentum, which is the product of the mass and velocity of an object. Velocity is defined as the rate of change of the position of an object. In everyday speech, mass is often synonymous with weight, but strictly speaking, weight means the strength of the gravitational pull on the object—how heavy it is measured in units of force.

We often talk about speed when we really mean velocity, and when we should be referring to momentum (which takes into account the mass we are trying to move). So, the sum of small movements every day across a large organization will have far greater impact than if a few people make great leaps of change.

es—especially changes they don't believe in or that require them to learn a new skill.

Pleasant Reassurance of New Words

Change leaders usually pay a great deal of attention to the words they use in announcing change with the misplaced belief that those words will translate to change success. They rarely do.

In a blog post (01/23/11) with the same title as this section, blogger and author Seth Godin wrote: "It's a lot easier for an organization to adopt new words than it is to actually change anything. Real change is uncomfortable. If it's not feeling that way, you've probably just adopted new words."

It is important to remember that as powerful as words can be, they usually need the strength of structural, process, governance, rewards, and recognition changes to bring them to reality.

Communicating What Has to Change

Changes in IT principles have implications for Business-IT governance processes, structures, and reporting. There may need to be new policies, changes to rewards and

---

Constancy of Purpose in Organizational Change

In his superb book, Good to Great: Why Some Companies Make the Leap… and Others Don't *(2001), Jim Collins introduced a flywheel analogy.*

In his research for the book, Collins learned that companies who make the transition don't do so overnight. He analogizes their success to that of a flywheel, where it is sustained momentum that accelerates the energy output and ultimately drives transformation.

This reminds me of the wisdom of the great sage of total quality, W. Edwards Deming and the first of his 14 points: constancy of purpose. *Deming suggested creating constancy of purpose for continual improvement of products and service to society, allocating resources to provide for long range needs rather than only short-term profitability, with a plan to become competitive, to stay in business, and to provide jobs.*

As I look at some clients I've worked with over the years, with their flavor of the month change programs, it is no wonder that they move backwards rather than forwards, and that their employees ignore strategic change initiatives by adopting a this too shall pass *attitude.*

Giving IT Principles Teeth: An Example

I was in a heated discussion with a client after we had completed an IT strategy refresh. One of the outstanding items was to review their IT principles. The IT leadership team had come up with some new candidate principles and I was asked if I thought they were appropriate.

I asked, "What will you do with these IT principles?" The silence I was met with was palpable. My client was too polite to say it, but I knew that in the silence he was thinking, "Vaughan, a principle is a principle! Having principles is the whole kahuna! It has nothing to do with what you do with them!

There are three keys to making IT principles valuable:
1. *Pick a few pain points you want to address. Typically these are significant performance inhibitors that surface time and again.*
2. *Come up with a principle that is a simple, direct, and unambiguous statement that FORCES A CHOICE that would resolve the pain point. The alternative choices should be viable. If one of them is not viable, then it's not a real choice. The test here is that a sane person could argue the opposite.*
3. *Identify what will have to change so that behaviors will change to come into alignment with the principle, then determine what it will take to change those behaviors.*

For example, you have frequent tension and debates around how much of the IT budget goes to maintenance. You've had good success getting prioritization of major new initiatives based on business value, but ongoing maintenance of existing solutions is nickel-and-diming you to death! You drill into root causes, ask a lot of whys (as described on the facing page), and eventually recognize that the planning for new initiatives never takes full lifecycle costs into account. This meets key #1 above. It's a real pain point.

You create a new IT principle: We manage all business solutions and technology investments based upon total value of ownership, including total life cycle benefits and costs. This meets key #2 above. A sane person could argue that we should not manage all business solutions based upon total value of ownership.

This is where I feared that my client was going to stop. It was going to feel good to the client's IT leadership team to draft the words in their principles, and perhaps print them on posters or as handy pocket inserts.

It seemed to them, that the words would change things somehow. They wouldn't. For real change to occur, we had to address key #3. What will have to change for us to act in accordance with this principle?

recognition, and modifications to IT audit procedures.

In the example of IT principles described on the facing page, supporting polices might include:

- The total cost of ownership of an IT asset and its value-contribution must be periodically calculated, and tracked over time. This requires closer alignment between program planning, project estimating, budgeting, and benefits tracking processes.
- The cost of a new system should include the cost to retire the system it replaces.
- Application retirement must be an active process.
- The total cost of ownership must include both business and technology costs of developing, deploying, and operating business solutions.
- Costs such as hardware, software, maintenance, security, monitoring, training, and on-going support must be included in the total cost of ownership.

The Problem with Conventional Change Management

There is a problem with conventional change management wisdom. In decades of the early and mid-industrial revolution, organizations were relatively simple and stable systems. Like machines, they were divided into functions and sub-functions, and they behaved somewhat linearly.

Strategy was formulated at the top of the hierarchy, work was performed at the bottom, with middle management interpreting between executives and workers. Assembly line folk did the work, and staff handled control and support functions. Power and

Root Cause Analysis using 5 Whys
Lack of consequences is a common issue in change failure.

I've had CIOs complain to me, "We aren't great at implementation and follow through!"

I typically get into the 5 Whys routine:"Why aren't you good at implementation?"

When they answer, I again ask "why?"

And I keep asking why after every answer until they tell me, "We don't hold people accountable." Or, "There are no consequences for them following through or not."

One more "why" from me usually gives them the mirror they need to see. They see and recognize the enemy.

information was smoothly transferred up and down the organization like cogs and chains.

This view is reflected in the mechanistic methods for organizational change that were popularized by researchers such as Kurt Lewin. Conventional wisdom held that if leadership wants small changes, then they should do incremental things at the lower parts of the organization. Large changes require radical interventions at higher levels. Even the traditional language of change speaks of unfreezing, refreezing, and resistance, as if describing a rusty or gummed up machine.

As information and knowledge replace minerals and machinery as industry's fuel, organizations are becoming increasingly complex and dynamic. The intuitive ways organizations were steered in simpler times no longer works.

Small interventions, such as 6 Sigma, agile, or lean manufacturing, can lead to massive change. Large interventions, such as business process re-engineering and restructuring often fail completely, as the organization springs back to its original form—like a motorcycle fork rebounding from a pothole.

Finding New IT Order in the Chaos

Today, there is a different way to handle change — one that goes with the flow rather than against it. Organizations are complex beasts, both in terms of the number of moving parts and the many subtle relationships. In scientific terms they are complex systems. This theory leads to a very different paradigm for effecting change.

An Organic Approach to Organizational Change

Those managing change in today's dynamic organizations must discard conventional wisdom. They must forget mechanistic images of the organization, recognize the inherent complexities, and draw, instead, from the sciences of chaos, complexity, and ecology.

For example chaos, with its strange attractors, explains why major interventions may lead to little or no change, while small changes can produce radical results—the *butterfly effect* suggested by mathematician and meteorologist Edward Lorenz. By approaching organizations as complex, dynamic organisms, rather than as machines, managers recognize that they can't predict the outcome to any given intervention.

Informed managers approach their change tasks in a more incremental, holistic, and organic fashion. They realize that they aren't really managing change in the conventional sense of the word. They are more sensitive to the complex interactions between systems, and use whole systems approaches that get as many stakeholders involved in the change as possible.

> *Shared vision and values become the genetic code that shapes behavior throughout the organization*

Shared vision and values become the *genetic code* that shapes behavior throughout the organization, rather than detailed change designs engineered from above. Information becomes a source of both order and creativity.

While the mechanistic approach treats work structures as permanent, and transition structures as temporary (pilot projects, change teams, and so on), the organic approach has fluid work structures (teams, self-organizing networks, defined capabilities), and permanent transition-support structures (social networks, communities of interest, coaches).

Mastering Three Fundamentally Different Value Propositions

IT Organizations have to deliver day-in, day-out on three very different value propositions:

- **Operational excellence** for IT infrastructure
- **Customer intimacy** for leveraging business unit IT
- **Product leadership/innovation** for exploiting business opportunities and new operating models made possible through emerging technologies

Fuzzy Organizational Boundaries

As if those complexities were not enough, the boundaries between the work of the IT organization and the businesses it serves are blurring and shifting. What used to be the official source of all things related to IT is now one of many sources—including self-service, the computer jockey who hangs out in the mail room, the Geek Squad, and the World Wide Web.

It seems that people can accomplish just about anything via the internet. However, for many of them, they have to go home to do it. In the office, some of the more important and potentially innovative things people want to do are blocked. While the IT organization's vision might say something about enabling the business, often IT feels more like a barrier.

Chaos and Change

Chaos sensitizes observers to look for patterns rather than rules. An example is found in supersonic flight where initial attempts to break the sound barrier resulted in mysterious crashes until someone discovered the different control dynamics that are required to travel safely at speeds above the speed of sound.

Chaos sensitizes observers to look for patterns rather than rules

To expand on Pirsig's observation (on the facing page), traditional scientific method has always been, at the very best, 20-20 hindsight. Scientific method is good for helping people see where they've been. It is good for helping people test the truth of what they think they know. But it can't tell people where they ought to go.

It is not surprising that the natural instinct of any IT leader is to try to control the chaos. However, the lens of complexity theory provides insights into more productive and less painful ways of managing than the draconian measures traditionally employed.

Organizations as Complex Adaptive Systems

Approaching IT organizations as complex adaptive systems (CAS) is a more effective paradigm for organizing and managing IT capabilities and for creating a new order

Zen, Motorcycles, and the Art of Organizational Change Management

I published an article in 1996 in Hewlett-Packard's Perspectives magazine. I include it here with minor updates.

In his book Zen and the Art of Motorcycle Maintenance *(1974), Robert Pirsig used a motorcycle as a metaphor to explore philosophy, quality, and the meaning of life. I'd like to extend the metaphor to examine the nature of organizational change and discuss why conventional change-management wisdom (which mostly surfaced in the last century) when applied to today's complex organizational context may lead you dangerously off course.*

The motorcycle is a machine, constructed from components, assemblies, and sub-assemblies. Power is generated in an engine or motor and transferred to a wheel through gears, cogs, and chains. We can understand this machine by describing its parts and how they fit together. The motorcycle behaves according to simple laws of Newtonian mechanics. If you want to turn left, you steer to the left.

Actually, that is not what happens. If you want to turn left, you must steer right! What looks like a simple machine operating according to predictable laws becomes a complex set of interacting systems that behave neither linearly nor intuitively. This is called countersteering and is the way to steer a motorcycle (or a bicycle). At low speeds, the effect is so subtle as to be virtually invisible. Most motorcyclists don't even know they are countersteering unless they have been trained to use countersteering to avoid becoming road kill. So why aren't bikers constantly careening off the road? Under normal conditions, this countersteering effect is very subtle. Ask a biker how he steers and he will say: "I lean." The reality is, the only way to lean at anything above parking-lot speeds is by applying subtle pressure to the handlebars in the direction opposite the intended turn.

The safest way to corner on a motorcycle is to countersteer into the turn and then gradually open the throttle through the turn. Constant throttle, or even worse, reducing the throttle in a turn (the intuitive thing to do) leads to wobbling and an unfortunate tendency to leave the road. This can be explained by Newton's first law—changing direction requires energy. If the energy of maneuvering a curve is not replaced by opening the throttle, the speed of the bike drops, the lean angle changes, and the bike becomes unstable. A biker can get by for years doing this unconsciously until there is an emergency and the hapless biker, who doesn't understand countersteering, is unable to turn sufficiently quickly to avoid a hazard.

Managing change is similar to riding motorcycles. Doing what seems intuitive gets you by until organizational complexity, or ambiguity of the change, reaches a certain pitch. The nuke the process, take no prisoners *re-engineering approach fails miserably, and expensively, because it assumes machine-like organizational qualities.*

out of the chaos. A CAS is a special case of complex systems.

Complex adaptive systems are complex in that they are diverse and made up of multiple interconnected elements. These relationships between components are intricate and lead to non-linear behavior. CAS are adaptive in that they have the capacity to change and learn from experience. Examples of CAS include ant colonies, the biosphere and the ecosystem, manufacturing businesses, and any human social group-based endeavor in a cultural and social system such as political parties or communities.

Features of Complex Adaptive Systems
Just like IT organizations, complex systems have boundaries that are hard to determine. They exhibit memory in that prior states may have an influence on present states. This effect can sometimes be seen as an organization's tendency to return to familiar patterns of behavior after being disturbed by an intervention such as a reorganization.

CAS behaviors emerge from a complex interaction between CAS components that can be impossible to predict. For example, social networks around a particular topic or issue can emerge without any specific effort to create such a network, while attempts to foster a given community might quickly fade away.

A small force can have a large impact. For decades, this has been called the *butterfly effect*. More recently, it is recognized as *going viral*. The term *Butterfly Effect* arises from Chaos Theory and, in particular, from a theory that suggested one flap of a bird's

---

Taylor's Scientific Management Was Blind to the Science of Complexity
Frederick Winslow Taylor's contributions to management theory were appropriate to his time (1856-1915). High productivity could be achieved by segregating mental work (planning and controlling) from physical work (manufacturing). People destined for mental work would be suitably trained. Those selected for physical work would be suitably incentivized.

In Taylor's time, companies were relatively simple. Most focused on the machinery of manufacturing and merchandising, so it was natural to treat the human systems as machine-like. Also, the scientific community had not yet developed the theoretical underpinnings of complex systems. Today, the science of complex adaptive systems is far more appropriate than the mechanistic, deterministic science of Frederick Taylor's time.

wings could alter the course of weather forever.

This theory became popularized with the bird being replaced by the more romantic *butterfly*. The bottom line: in CAS, small changes can have massive, unpredictable effects, while large changes might have little or no effect, and might even lead to unintended and undesirable consequences.

The CAS paradigm presents a far more realistic perspective on IT organizational behavior than does the deterministic view that has dominated organizational design for the past fifty years or so. In today's emerging Web 2.0 world, IT needs to be managed as a complex and organic capability, rather than through functional organization designs with their lines and boxes.

The Nature of Fractals

One useful notion from complexity science is the fractal. A fractal is a shape that can be split into parts, each of which is (at least approximately) a copy of the whole at a reduced scale. This property is called self-similarity.

Fractals, like the one shown below, have a simple and recursive definition that underlies their self-similarity. The way the tree trunk leads to major branches leading to smaller branches, is an example of self-similarity. The leaves on a tree are similar to each other, although no two leaves are identical. Similar patterns occur throughout

Example of a Fractal

nature. Patterns seen in rivers and streams are similar to those found in human bronchial tubes. The alveoli structures in human lungs are very similar to the structures of broccoli.

The fractal shown on the previous page is composed of dozens of small blue triangles of similar structure. These triangles can be equated to the underlying enabling capabilities that influence the value chain in an organization. Each alignment of triangles is replicated at an increasingly larger scale.

As the fractal replicates, and the patterns it creates become more complex, white triangles seem to emerge and dominate the graphic, even though the underlying shape and characteristics of the primary blue triangle, and the rules that govern the structure of the fractal remain unchanged.

Fractals: The Lego Blocks of Organization Design

Fractals can be thought of as Lego pieces. Legos are easy to assemble and disassemble. They comprise a set of standard shapes, with standard connectors. This endows them with relatively predictable behaviors, including the ability to

Patterns repeat in organizations like organizational fractals

easily reconfigure shapes. Patterns repeat in organizations like organizational fractals. Examples include:

- Self-organizing teams
- Centers of expertise (or centers of competence)
- Project management capabilities
- Program management capabilities
- Service management capabilities
- Product management capabilities
- Relationship management capabilities

The Fractal Nature of IT Capabilities

All decompositions of IT capabilities will have a similar structure—a primary value chain drawing upon underlying enabling capabilities, and influenced by alignment and governance capabilities. Organizational fractals can be a useful approach to organization design when a four-step (fractal) process is followed:

1. Encourage the creation of self-organizing teams
2. Give them a common purpose
3. Let them arrive at a few simple rules of engagement
4. Get out of their way

Providing the Genetic Code That Allows Fractal Structures to Collaborate

The traditional, mechanistic model of organizational change led from the top-down is gradually being replaced with a more organic, emergent, and collaborative approach to leading change. For fractal organizational structures to collaborate toward attaining common goals, it is essential that they share a genetic code through:

- Shared goals
- Common vision
- Open communication across porous boundaries

With these attributes as a context, fractal organizational structures can be an extremely effective way to create an IT organization with capabilities that adapt to the environment, and self-correct in response to external or internal forces. These IT capabilities aren't always within an IT organization. IT capabilities can exist anywhere inside or external to an enterprise with porous boundaries.

Creating Collaborative Culture With Wikis

The inherent tendency to prevent bad change creates tough dilemmas when introducing social networking and collaboration capabilities such as Wikis. Wikis thrive best where the culture is open and emergent—enabling good change.

The inherent tendency to prevent bad change creates tough dilemmas

Designers of the governance mechanisms for a Wiki have some interesting choices. For example:

- Do they allow people to create their own pages or do they put controls on who creates and who edits pages?
- Do they allow all spaces to be open to anyone in the organization or do they allow for private spaces, where a select few (such as an IT leadership team) collaborate?
- Do they allow people to display avatars that are humorous or ironic or do they insist on corporate photographs from people's security badges?
- Do they allow people to write in their unique voices—even if a little rough around the edges—or do they have a *Wiki Gardener* monitor pages and clean up the rough edges?

IT leadership can take the position that Wiki governance should be designed for the current state: "We are locked down, deeply concerned about security and privacy. We have to have special standards of conduct and controls to keep things structured and secure."

Changing the Culture of an IT Organization One Wiki Page at a Time

I've been a student of IT organizational culture since I began my management consulting career some 40+ years ago. It's wrong, of course, to generalize too broadly, but I've worked with literally hundreds of large enterprise IT organizations (i.e., IT organizations of 250+ members) and have seen more commonalities than differences.

Naturally, there are sub-cultures within any IT organization (e.g., architects are not the same as operations people or as solution developers), but these sub-cultures, like all fractal organization structures, have more similarities than sharp differences.

Technology can be either an enabler or inhibitor of organizational change. I've found that by breaking down the boundaries between sub-cultures, and allowing fractal organizational structures to collaborate freely, a well-managed Wiki can be a powerful enabler of change.

Or IT leadership can take the position that governance should be designed with an eye to the desired future state: "We encourage open dialog and a thriving community of adults. Keep within our corporate code of integrity and help make the Wiki a safe, valuable, and fun place to grow and share our enterprise knowledge about IT."

When people responsible for approving Wiki governance do not have significant experience with a more open model, their inclination will be to play it safe, and design for the current state. Unfortunately, that is likely to perpetuate the current culture and probably prevent the Wiki from becoming what it was intended to become.

It may take one or two strong, visionary leaders to make a leap of faith and allow a governance model that reflects higher aspirations for IT and corporate culture.

Afterword: Leadership Lessons From The Performing Arts

In today's hectic, multitasking world, it's hard to carve out time for learning

Vaughan Merlyn at Rock 'n' Roll Fantasy Camp

Overview

This Afterword taps my favorite hobby—performing in a rock 'n roll band—and it draws out twenty lessons from my experience in the performing arts that can be applied to IT Organizational Leadership and Management.

Afterword: Leadership Lessons From The Performing Arts

Leadership Lessons from Rock 'n' Roll

A while ago I took advantage of being between consulting engagements to take some personal time to indulge my alter ego. While my *Dr. Jekyll* is a relatively staid and introverted management consultant and educator, I have a *Mr. Hyde* lurking inside me who loves nothing more than to strap on a guitar, plug into a powerful sound system, and make musical mayhem!

I discovered an outlet for my alter ego in 2005. I was looking forward to a sabbatical when I saw a segment about Rock 'n' Roll Fantasy Camp on a "Fine Living Channel" broadcast on a Delta flight. I signed up for the camp and it literally changed my life! In the next few pages I'll share some lessons learned from my experiences that I think can be applied to the world of IT management.

Five Days that Changed My World

That 5-day rock camp in Hollywood, CA in 2005 had me playing with rock stars including Roger Daltrey (The Who), Jon Anderson (Yes), Dickey Betts (The Allman Brothers), Elliot Easton (The Cars), and many more. I was teamed up with five other campers. We were assigned a counselor—Kelly Keagy, drummer, singer, and song-writer from the band Night Ranger. Kelly was the creative and singing force behind the rock classic anthem, "Sister Christian," and many other hits.

Our band went to hell and back during the course of a long week, rehearsing from morning till night, jamming with other campers and counselors, and learning about song writing and the music business in master classes led by the counselors.

With Roger Daltrey from The Who at the Hollywood House of Blues

We also learned some fabulous lessons in performance from Kelly. For example, if a band looks like it's having fun, so will the audience. If a band looks nervous and uncomfortable, the audience will sense it and will responds with less enthusiasm.

At the risk of stating the obvious, this is equally true in any setting. If you act nervous and tentative, you will have a hard time establishing your credibility and engaging and persuading an audience. It has to be fun!

Lesson 1
Enjoy yourself!
If you are having fun, so will your audience (team or clients).
If you are nervous and uncomfortable, your audience will sense it
and will respond with less enthusiasm.

The week culminated in a live performance and a *battle of the bands* at the Hollywood House of Blues on the famous Sunset Strip. The experience was truly incredible—made all the more special when our band won the battle of the bands, thanks to Kelly's remarkable coaching skills.

The camp was featured on "Good Morning America" the morning following the House of Blues performance, much to the amusement of several observant business colleagues who saw the GMA segment. They had simply been told I was on vacation. (I was rather secretive about my alter ego back then!)

The whole camp had also been filmed by "The Learning Channel." It aired as a two-hour documentary later that year to the surprise of many of my consulting clients who happened to see the TV show, its promos, or its re-runs.

Dr. Jekyll, Meet Mr. Hyde
It is always amazing to me how apparently unconnected things can suddenly intersect and create new opportunities! Throughout the several weeks it took to come down from the high of the 2005 Rock 'n' Roll Fantasy Camp, I'd been reflecting on how much I'd learned at the camp, and what a fantastic incubator for team building it had proven to be.

I realized how much more refreshed I felt and how much more effective I was in my day job. As a bonus, I found myself with several ideas about how to build on the camp concept and increase the opportunities for people to take advantage of this amazing experience.

I approached David Fishof, the camp's founder, producer, and chief executive. We agreed to meet in New York. David's immediate reaction at the meeting was that some of my ideas were probably unworkable, but that others had merit. I began working with David on a business plan to expand the camp. Soon I found myself meeting with Hollywood producers in Bel Air mansions, and all sorts of interesting characters from the entertainment industry.

Primarily due to David's genius as a music producer and promoter, the resulting camp expansion has been successful—with a TV reality series, regional camps, corporate camps (think about bringing one to your corporate training/motivational event), and a UK based camp that featured one week of recording at the hallowed Abbey Road Studios in London (where the Beatles and Pink Floyd recorded their masterpieces). The UK camp was capped by performances at a Soho, London club and, finally, at The Cavern in Liverpool.

I have now participated in multiple Rock 'n' Roll Fantasy Camps, playing in Las Vegas, New York, Los Angeles, and even in an experimental one-day camp where we opened for Journey and Def Leppard at a stadium show in Columbus, OH. My latest saga was recording at Abbey Road.

On the Massive Console in Abbey Road's Studio 3

Lessons in Learning, Team Building, and Organizational Change

I learned several lessons from my Rock Camp experiences that can be applied in team building and organizational change.

The Value of Risk Taking

For many of us, most of the time, fear of failure is a huge inhibitor to success. Sometimes it manifests itself, strangely, as fear of success. In my first camp in 2005, I found myself in a band with three guitarists but no bass player. I had played guitar before, but the bass is a very different instrument.

The bass typically has fewer strings, but a much longer neck, meaning the fret positions your hands have learned over years of playing no longer work. Less obvious, but a huge unexpected insight to me, was that the bass should be approached as a rhythm section instrument because it has more in common with the drums than the melodies of the song.

Lesson 2

*Most of the time, fear of failure is a huge inhibitor to success.
Sometimes it manifests itself, strangely, as fear of success.*

Having never played a bass guitar, I volunteered to take bass duties on our first song with reluctance. I discovered, much to my horror, that we were to open our stage show at The House of Blues with an old Animals song, "We Gotta Get Outta This Place!" This blues classic begins with a well-known bass riff, so screwing that up would be horribly noticeable!

Lesson 3
Dealing with change and seizing opportunities are all about taking risks. Be prepared to make a fool of yourself and damn the consequences!

As a result of taking this risk, I've come to love bass guitar, and have played the bass with bands outside of the camps in Chicago, New York, Atlanta, London, and Liverpool. I even played on a cruise ship.

I've found that demand for bass players seems perpetually high, and I've learned to listen to music differently than I did before trying my hand at bass. Best of all, I learned to be less intimidated by risk taking.

With Slash from Guns 'n Roses

The Value of Forming, Storming, Norming, Performing

In 1965 Bruce Tuckman introduced the concept that teams develop through four stages: forming (agreeing on goals and beginning tasks), storming (building trust—often through conflict), norming (resolving disagreements and beginning to cooperate), and performing (acting on common goals). Each step is important for team building including storming—the sometimes disagreeable one.

Lesson 4
The forming, storming, norming, and performing homily of team building is not only true, each step is essential.

If you think you can bypass the *storming* stage, you are wrong. You simply have not yet bonded as a team. And if you think you can skip directly from *forming* to *performing*, you will find yourself *storming* during a performance.

I had one camp experience where we all seemed to gel. The band members had common musical tastes, similar skill levels, and seemed to genuinely hit it off. While several in our band suspected there might be some issues to work out with our vocalist, we hoped to finesse rather than confront the situation. Wrong! During our first stage performance at a London night club, our singer experienced a panic attack, stormed off the stage and out of the club! We weren't quite as bonded and comfortable with each other as I'd believed.

Lesson learned: teams have to go through the four stages. If you have not had disputes and differences of opinion in your team (or band or whatever), it's because you have not yet uncovered them, or are too polite to confront them. Hidden just below the surface, these dysfunctions lie waiting to trip you up—often at the worst possible moment!

The Value of The Learning Process

For me, most learning takes place when I can immerse myself in the learning experience. Regrettably, in today's hectic, multitasking world, it's hard to carve out time for learning.

Lesson 5
Learning is exhausting and exhilarating!
It takes tremendous energy, focus, and the courage to get through a variety of setbacks.

I know there will be periods of forward progress when anything seems possible, and horribly dark periods, when it all seems like a lost cause and a waste of everybody's time. But with real commitment and focus, great things are possible, even from mere mortals with very limited musical talent.

A couple of years ago I was in a camp band with Teddy (*Zigzag*) Andreadis, who had toured with Guns 'n Roses (among other major bands). Furthermore, Slash, the exceptional guitarist from Guns 'n Roses, was going to be joining us in the studio. We decided to learn "Paradise City"—a choice agreed to before I realized how challenging some of the bass lines were. They were, seemingly, beyond my humble abilities. However, I worked at it, and within a few hours I had the part nailed. Even Slash complimented my bass part.

Some months later, our band from that camp decided to play a reunion gig in New York at Arlene's Grocery in Soho. "No problem!" I thought. Then to my horror, when preparing for the New York performance, I found I could not play the part! I went back to the video from that camp to prove to myself that it had not been a dream and that I really had played the bass lines! Knowing that gave me the confidence to try again, and to experience a very successful and rewarding performance in New York.

Lesson learned? Learning takes tremendous energy, focus, and the courage to get

With Teddy Andreadis from Guns 'n Roses at
the Hollywood House of Blues

through a variety of setbacks. Don't agree to learn a new skill unless you are prepared to immerse yourself and to commit the time and tenacity to do it properly!

What I Learned About IT Management From My Musical Sabbatical

One of the gifts I'm enjoying in my semi-retirement is more time pursuing my musical hobbies, including performing with local musicians and friends. That creative outlet reinforces for me, at the deepest level, how much good musical performance demands intense listening.

Lesson 6
Superior performance demands intense listening!

Intense listening is extremely relevant to my professional world of IT management consulting as well. The client challenge, as presented, is rarely the real challenge. Consultants have to listen through all the noise to hear what is really going on. They also have to listen with their eyes to see what is really going on. This means watching the body language of IT leaders and influencers.

Lesson 7
Avoid listening deficiency syndrome. For superb listening,
listen through all the noise with your ears to hear what's going on and
listen with your eyes to see what is going on.

Much of my work is with CIOs—people who are often, by definition, very bright, innovative, and even charismatic characters. Yet I frequently see *listening deficiency syndrome*. This is a failure to actually hear what is going on around them. If consultants are not skilled at hearing what their audience is saying, they cannot be skilled at selling them the next IT enablement opportunity.

Web 2.0 is largely about collaboration. Collaboration demands superb listening skills—listening very broadly—with the eyes as well as with the ears.

There's a wealth of available material about listening skills so I don't intend to make this a guide for improving listening skills. But I do want to share some personal insights that have mostly come to me through my hobbies.

I guess there is a mini-insight even in that sentence. Active hobbies are really important to a healthy mind! I often work with client IT professionals who are locked into ten-hour days that flow into weekends. They are trying to get on top of email in-boxes with thousands of unread messages. When they say they don't have time for hobbies, I fear for their sanity and for their effectiveness! I consider hobbies to be non-optional—period!

Lesson 8
Active hobbies are important for maintaining a healthy mind, sanity, and effectiveness.

Lessons Learned from Music and Performing

As I've tried to learn music over the years (starting with the guitar when I was about ten) I've come to appreciate the importance of listening, and how hard it is to listen when you are focused on trying to play the right notes. More importantly and more challenging, when playing music with others, the natural tendency is to focus on what you are playing and to listen to how you are sounding. I quickly learned that it's less about what you play, and more about what you hear!

The real trick is to focus on the other instruments and voices—what they are playing and how they are sounding! With focus and concentration, you can hear any given part by effectively filtering out the other parts.

Lesson 9
Filtering, focus, and attention are important skills in deep and active listening!

The lesson here is, whether in music or in discussing the business value of an IT solution, filtering, focus, and attention are important skills in deep and active listening! Think how this lesson might apply to CIO and CTO roles. Are they talking about their own domains, or about each other's? How do they refer to customers, clients, business partners, and their staff? Do they have a balanced approach to their world, or does it tend to be narrow and biased? Think about how that might apply to your role versus those of your colleagues?

Lessons from Acting and Dramatics

I learned a wonderful lesson as a teenager when I got involved in amateur dramatics. Just as with the music experience, the natural tendency is to focus on your own lines—what *you* are saying. The trick, I soon learned, was to listen to the other actors and, more importantly, to the audience!

I learned this the hard way. My first big play was a wonderful comedy—"You Can't

Take It With You"—by George S. Kaufman and Moss Hart. Through weeks of rehearsal, we had a pretty good sense of the funny lines and how to deliver them. We then got to the actual week of performances. Everything went well for the first and second nights. On the third night, something very strange happened. I delivered one of the non-funny lines, and the entire audience roared with laughter!

Without warning, a straight line that I'd delivered the same way over weeks of rehearsals was suddenly funny—not just to a few audience members, but to the whole audience! I suddenly got a joke that neither I nor other members of the cast had ever seen before.

When we debriefed after the performance, we all agreed that the line was indeed funny, but that we had not recognized its humor until that moment in the third live performance in front of an audience.

This experience taught me a great deal about the challenges of comedic timing. Intense listening is important even as you struggle to remember your next line and how to deliver it! If you aren't ready for the laughter, you will talk over it and the audience will miss some lines. Even worse, if you are expecting laughter and briefly pause the performance while waiting for the laughter, you've interrupted the flow and momentarily broken the illusion that good theater hangs on.

The other lesson here is to listen to the pace and rhythm of your audience and try to match that.

Lesson 10
In life, as in art, pacing is everything.
Listen to the pace and rhythm of your audience and try to match it.

More Leadership Lessons from the Performing Arts

I'm passionate about music—both as a listener, and as an amateur performer. As a listener, my tastes are broad. I grew up in a house where the music of Tchaikovsky, Bach, Stravinsky, and Beethoven were a constant source of inspiration and enrichment. My teenage years in London in the early 60s meant that The Who, Rolling Stones, and others of that era, were the bands that I danced to in local clubs and pubs.

My university years introduced me to the richer and more complex music of classical and psychedelic rock (Yes and Pink Floyd, and other titans played at our student union gigs). As an amateur performer, my preferred genre has been Rock 'n Roll and

With Chris Squire and Jon Davison from Yes and our Rock 'n' Roll Fantasy Camp Band

blues. It's easier for mere mortals to get involved in a performance of a Guns 'n Roses or AC/DC song than it is with Stravinsky's Rite of Spring.

Through my opportunities to participate in several Rock 'n' Roll Fantasy Camps, I've noticed that most professional musicians are multi-talented. They are not the one trick ponies you might imagine them to be.

One of the first stars I got to play with was Simon Kirke, drummer extraordinaire from Free and Bad Company. I was amazed to see such a strong drummer pick up a guitar and be highly accomplished on that instrument—then a bass, then keyboards.

My first band counselor was Kelly Keagy, drummer and singer from 80s arena rock band Night Ranger, and best known as the singer and composer of the power ballad "Sister Christian." It was the same story. Kelly could play any instrument really well, and was a wonderful producer and counselor.

Most recently, Teddy (*ZigZag*) Andreadis, best known as keyboard player for Guns 'N Roses, was my band's counselor. Like the others, Teddy could play anything. When we played at the House of Blues in Las Vegas, he actually played Hammond organ and guitar, and sang *at the same time*. (Don't ask me how. I don't know even though I was there and saw it!)

When I think about consummate professionals, I think of these highly talented musicians, and their determination to learn as much about music, performance, production, and recording as they can—not just to master one instrument. They have a passion for music. It's not just a job. They often stretch their talents beyond music into the arts. For example, John Lennon, Grace Slick, Ron Wood, and Jon Entwhistle were all accomplished artists.

There are similar examples in the other performing arts. The people we most enjoy, take risks and keep growing. (Consider Johnny Depp in the remarkable Sweeney Todd musical movie).

Lesson 11
If you want to be an IT leader as we head towards the future, open your horizons, take risks, keep learning! Most importantly, bring passion into your work.

This experience has a bearing on how I view IT leadership. I believe that IT professionals who thrive will be similarly multi-talented—technologist, business process engineer, modeler, communicator, collaborator, and visionary.

The lesson? If you want to be an IT leader as we head towards the future, open your horizons, take risks, keep learning! Most importantly, bring passion into your work.

Lessons in Humanity From One of the World's Leading Record Producers

At a recent Rock Camp in Los Angeles, I jammed with Ginger Baker (Cream, etc.), David Crosby (Crosby, Stills and Nash, etc.), and a host of top musicians from Steely Dan, Guns 'n' Roses, Black Sabbath, Quiet Riot, Kiss, Grand Funk Railroad, and more.

As I described earlier, in the Rock 'n' Roll Fantasy Camp program, you are assigned to a band, have a genuine rock star counselor to rehearse with, and perform at top venues (Whisky A Go Go and Lucky Strike).

In addition to this, our band had opted for the recording package that included a day (which turned out to be a ten-hour day!) in a top recording studio with the legendary

With Nick Mason from Pink Floyd and my wife, Gillian

producer Eddie Kramer—who worked with artists such as the Beatles, David Bowie, Eric Clapton, Jimi Hendrix, The Kinks, Kiss, Led Zeppelin, the Rolling Stones and Carlos Santana.

Working with our little band, Strange Crew, was probably a unique challenge for Eddie, but he took on the challenge and rose to the occasion! The band members, who had never met before, were together for three days of forming, storming, norming, and performing under the wonderful counseling of Kane Roberts , Alice Cooper's lead guitarist.

It was an intriguing and ultimately rewarding experience and an exceptionally enjoyable way to develop new competencies and capabilities!. It was, at the same time, both humbling and life-affirming.

Lessons Learned From My Recording Experience
In this section, I'll focus on lessons learned from my recording experience. There are many additional lessons from my rehearsing and from performances at Hollywood's hallowed music clubs, but I've covered those elsewhere.

Lesson 12
Emotional Intelligence trumps all else!

Emotional intelligence (sometimes called EQ) is the ability to express emotions and empathy. It is now generally recognized as a more accurate predictor of career success than IQ, or just about any other personal characteristic.

I would say that Eddie's EQ is through the roof! I don't know if he learned this through years of working with egomaniacs, alcoholics, and drug addicts, or if he was born with an innate ability to work with diverse individuals and groups, but his mastery in this regard was clear throughout the day.

For example:
- Eddie handled each of us band members using very different inter-personal styles. He was able to quickly read us and relate to each of us in ways that were comfortable, appropriate, and effective. As an illustration, he had spent much of his life in the UK (where I am from), and very quickly established a rapport with me based on our shared roots. He recognized that I enjoy and use humor extensively, so he mirrored that behavior, quoting great British comics from my youth. For example, when he did not like the way I was approaching a lick, he'd stroll out of the control room, across the lengthy expanse of the main studio, and say, "not like this, like that!" (mimicking British comic/magician, Tommy Cooper).
- He knew when and how to cajole, to encourage, and to re-direct. He could easily have spoken his instructions through the control room microphone—a disembodied voice into the main studio. More often than not, he walked into the studio and came right up to the band member he was coaching, made direct eye contact, and gave clear instructions in ways that resonated with each of us.
- Eddie was always encouraging. If he had a criticism of the way one of us had played a certain part, he would usually contrast that criticism with a positive reinforcement. At one point he came out of the control room to tell our drummer, "I loved the way you played the chorus section. It was brilliant! So, I'm wondering why you aren't playing the verses that way?"
- When his frustration with a recording engineer or band member was getting to him, Eddie walked over to a grand piano and played classical music very skillfully! He recognized his frustration button was being pushed, recognized that he needed to control this, and knew from experience that a few minutes at the piano keyboard would help restore his cool.
- Kane Roberts also demonstrated high EQ in the ways he coached us. In fact, I've found from previous Rock 'n' Roll Fantasy Camp experiences that the counselors are selected, not only for their musical talent and pedigree, but for their coaching abilities.

Lesson 13
Preparation is everything!
Take time to nail the preparation so you can give your best performance.
You often only have one take in life (and in business), so make it count!

Of the grueling ten hours in the studio, three hours were consumed getting the re-corded sounds just right. Yes, one-third of the time was getting all the equipment set up—especially the microphones surrounding the drum set.

- There's an adage I remember from my early years: There's never time to do it right, but you always find time to do it over! I know we are in a fast-moving world, and that speed matters. But, depending on the context, quality some-times matters more. To spend seven hours recording only to find out later that the sound was off would mean several more hours of retakes and editing. By then we'd have all been well past our best.
- Take time to nail the preparation so you can give your best performance, be it an important presentation, meeting facilitation, or whatever.
- You often only have one take in life so make it count!

Lesson 14
Don't underestimate the importance of the support crew!
Value them, nurture them, and train them to do their roles.

Eddie Kramer is a genius, and undoubtedly one of the most successful and talented producers/engineers in the business. But he also depends upon assistants, as we all do in our professional careers.

- Pick your support crew carefully. Value them, nurture them, train them, help them understand their place in the performance.
- Recognize them when they do something the way you want.
- Correct them when they don't and explain why you are correcting them.

Lesson 15
Always be fully present!
Today's pace and habits have us all multi-tasking.
This might feel smart and productive but it's not!

This is something I think I knew as a student, but somehow forgot (or ignored) once I had to face the demands of my career, in particular and life, in general. The need to keep many balls in the air in my work, and the emergence of tools and technologies with the power to enable multi-tasking, led me down a somewhat destructive path.

While live performances, by definition, have all the band members playing together, the recording process uses a mix of ensemble and solo performances. For any single band member, there can be a lot of sitting around, waiting—I would describe studio recording as 98% boredom and 2% sheer terror!

When you are needed, you have to be there mentally as well as physically, to understand exactly what has gone before, and what is expected of you next.

- You have to be ready to go at a moment's notice. Even when you aren't on, you have to behave as though you are.
- It's hard work not tuning out, but that's what it takes when you are part of a team.
- Each team member takes his or her turn, but you all have to be present the entire time.
- Staying present is easier to do (though not easy!) when you are physically together, less easy to do on a video conference, and very hard to do on a teleconference. How many times have you been on a conference call when a question is asked of someone and it is clear they weren't listening? How does that make the other members of the call feel? How much rework does it create?

The reality is that most of us have gotten into the habit of multi-tasking—talking on the phone while sending emails, for example. And more often than not, our work suffers. If it is routine, purely physical work, that might be OK. If it is more complex, that might not be OK. If it involves learning, it almost certainly is not OK. Do yourself a favor. Stop trying to move so fast and start trying to move effectively and deliberately.

If, heaven forbid, you needed brain surgery, how would you feel if you knew the brain surgeon was going to do the surgery while checking Facebook, talking with a golf buddy, and responding to emails?

Lesson 16
Take the time to shift gears occasionally!
Switching contexts helps sharpen key skills and develop new competencies.

Performing in a band, or working in a recording studio, is completely different from what I do most of the time. But my hobbies feed my professional domain in powerful and often unexpected ways:

- There are skills that transfer between my professional domain and my hobbies.
- Switching contexts helps me sharpen key skills and develop new competencies.
- Always look for new lessons you can apply in your work.
- Take time out to play—to do things purely for the fun of it.
- Recognize and sharpen skills that transfer from your professional life to your hobbies and vice versa.

Lessons on Multi-tasking

Lessons from Scuba Diving

I started scuba diving in 1995. Once again, the learning was as a middle-aged adult. My scuba learning experience was very much about single-tasking. You tend not to multi-task as a scuba diver—especially while you are learning. This is an easy conclusion to reach. Your life depends upon it!

As a learning diver, there's quite a lot to think about, and much of it has to do with avoiding death or some very nasty injuries. (Exploding lungs or eyeballs are difficult conditions to treat!). Lots of deep focus is required (excuse the pun). It is fine to learn how to take underwater photographs or videos once you have experience. Until you have mastered basic scuba skills, however, you tend not to do that.

Lesson 17
Don't multi-task.
Your life (or your business) might depend on staying focused.

Lessons from Motor Cycling

I had a similar mid-life learning experience with motorcycling. I had a motorbike as a teenager, but stopped riding until about 25 years ago when I got back into it. I took the Motorcycle Safety Foundation course which taught me a lot I did not know, including:

1. Most car, bus and truck drivers have not seen you on a motorcycle.
2. Some of those that do see you want to kill you!
3. There's a mental mantra that helps keep motorcyclists alive—Scan, Identify, Predict, Decide and Act (SIPDE is the mnemonic to help remember this mantra).

Survival means keeping a total focus on this mantra—a behavior I still practice today, even when driving a car. It becomes a kind of Zen thing. How many potentially dangerous situations can you see coming and be ready to deal with them?

Lesson 18
Scan, Identify, Predict, Decide and Act.
Watch for potentially dangerous situations and be ready to deal with them.

Lessons from the Performing Arts

I started playing guitar at about ten, then gave it up when I went to university. By then I had accepted that I was probably not going to make it as a professional musician and, therefore, needed to get a professional degree. I got back into music in 2005, so much of my professional development as a musician (I use that term very loosely, with tongue planted firmly in cheek), has come in the last fifteen years.

I once had to learn the bass guitar parts to five incredibly long and complex progressive rock compositions by the band Yes. I had to perform these in front of a large audience of Yes fans (where fan equals fanatic). I also had to play these in front of members of the band Yes and, in rehearsals, I had to play with members of Yes!

Among the five songs was one piece of over twenty minutes in duration with many key changes, changes in time signature, bass solos, very fast runs, and a host of challenges for a non-professional like me!

I started my usual practice routine, but it wasn't working or, at least, it wasn't working quickly enough. After a couple of weeks practice for an hour each evening, I thought hard about why I was not making the progress I needed.

The reason came to me when I was reading a blog post on multi-tasking. I realized that, as important as this performance was to me, I wasn't approaching my practice with the right mindset and focus. I was working hard at trying to get through the music, rather than feeling it, understanding it and really learning it. My head had been full of other issues I allowed to distract me.

I determined to take a different approach:
1. I needed a clear break between my work and my practice. In some cases that was fifteen minutes meditation. In other cases, it was time in my gym to exercise or to take a walk.
2. Each time I started a practice session, I had a specific learning objective—one small piece that I would loop and play over and over. I played each one slowly at first, then gradually came up to performance speed.
3. I kept a record of what I was working on and how I was doing.

4.   I turned off all other distractions—email, cell phone, office phone, etc.
5.   My mantra was FOCUS!

Within a couple of weeks, I saw real progress. Focus was paying off. I was seeing patterns in the music I had not seen before—patterns that helped with the learning process. I was seeing patterns in my playing—how one particularly tricky solo was actually in just two playing positions on the guitar neck.

Once I visualized the musical patterns and the playing positions, everything clicked. Suddenly, playing that solo was as natural as it could be. Suddenly it all made sense!

Lesson 19
Look for patterns. Patterns help with learning.

Van Halen, M&Ms, and Operational Excellence

One of the things I love about the rock music scene is the legends—some apocryphal, some based on fact—that surround many rock stars. One that's been around a while is the legend of the brown M&Ms associated with early Van Halen. I was delighted to come across a piece in *Fast Company* by Chip and Dan Heath that dug beneath the surface of this urban rock legend.

Van Halen toured extensively and used a tremendous amount of heavy equipment. All this gear, together with stage settings, special lighting and effects, needs a convoy of eighteen-wheel tractor trailers to haul it from gig to gig. Assembling and taking down all this equipment means high technical complexity, and demands a detailed and complex contract with venues and specialist resources.

One of the strange articles Van Halen buried in the middle of the contract read: There will be no brown M&Ms in the backstage area, upon pain of forfeiture of the show with no compensation.

When front man (and operational excellence obsessive) David Lee Roth would arrive at a new venue, he would go backstage to check the M&M bowl. If he saw a brown M&M, he took this as a visible indicator that the stage hands and venue specialists were not paying attention to the contract details, and there was a good chance that other operational errors had been made. This would trigger a line check of the entire production.

Twenty Lessons for Organizational Leadership

1. *Enjoy yourself! If you are having fun, so will your audience (team or clients) If you are nervous and uncomfortable, your audience senses it and will respond with less enthusiasm.*

2. *Most of the time, fear of failure is a huge inhibitor to success. Sometimes it manifests itself, strangely, as fear of success.*

3. *Dealing with change and seizing opportunities are all about taking risks. Be prepared to make a fool of yourself and damn the consequences.*

4. *The forming, storming, norming, and performing homily of team building is not only true, each step is essential.*

5. *Learning is exhausting and exhilarating. It takes tremendous energy, focus, and the courage to get through a variety of setbacks.*

6. *Superior performance demands intense listening.*

7. *Avoid listening deficiency syndrome. For superb listening, listen with your ears through all the noise to hear what's going on, and listen with your eyes to see what is going on.*

8. *Active hobbies are important for maintaining a healthy mind, sanity, and effectiveness.*

9. *Filtering, focus, and attention are important skills in deep and active listening!*

10. *In life, as in art, pacing is everything. Listen to the pace and rhythm of your audience and try to match it.*

11. *If you want to be an IT leader as we head towards the future, open your horizons, take risks, keep learning! Most importantly, bring passion into your work.*

12. *Emotional Intelligence trumps all else.*

13. *Preparation is everything! Take time to nail the preparation so you can give your best performance. You often only have one take in life (and in business), so make it count.*

14. *Don't underestimate the importance of the support crew! Value them, nurture them, and train them to do their roles.*

15. *Always be fully present! Today's pace and habits have us all multi-tasking. This might feel smart and productive but it's not.*

16. *Take the time to shift gears occasionally! Switching contexts helps sharpen key skills and develop new competencies.*

17. *Don't multi-task. Your life (or your business) might depend on staying focused.*

18. *Scan, Identify, Predict, Decide and Act. Watch for potentially dangerous situations and be ready to deal with them.*

19. *Look for patterns. Patterns help with learning.*

20. *When your work demands operational excellence, make sure everyone involved knows and understands the indicators that provide assurance of the quality of your operations.*

David Lee Roth had come up with a simple indicator to predict the quality of the stage set up for any venue and show. It looked trivial and something you might expect from a rock diva. In practice, it was a highly effective way to assure quality. You can bet that the word quickly spread from gig to gig, so that crews were on their toes, paying attention to all the contract details!

Lesson 20
When your work demands operational excellence, make sure everyone involved knows and understands the indicators that provide assurance of the quality of your operations.

What's your equivalent to the brown M&Ms? Do you have any indicators that provide assurance of the quality of your operations?

Biography: How My Career Frames My Worldview

I was born in London in 1947, one block from the famous Portobello Road street market. This was a time of food rationing and playing around the many bomb sites that littered London.

Portobello Road, North Kensington, London, UK (Around 1953)

My fifty-year career in IT has taken me through three distinct phases. Each phase created a different lens through which I perceived the shifting IT management landscape.

Phase 1—Engineer

I've had engineering inclinations for as long as I can remember. I was an electronics hobbyist as a teen, repairing electrical and electronic appliances (radios, televisions, etc.) for pocket money. I was also a keen mechanic, rebuilding car and motorcycle engines and transmissions.

In 1966 I entered an innovative (for its time) BSc Electrical Engineering *sandwich course* in the UK. This four-year program comprised eight, six-month sessions, alternating between university and industry. In the industry *slices* of the sandwich, I designed digital and analog computers for Crosfield Electronics, a company that built imaging automation for the printing industry. This company sponsored my BSc course at Salford University and moved me among four major departments (research and development, engineering, manufacturing and marketing) over the four years.

In 1970, with my freshly minted electrical engineering degree, I joined International Computers, Limited (ICL) as a Systems Engineer. At the time, ICL was Britain's largest computer company. As part of this job, I went through six months of outstanding residential training in business and systems.

However, I soon lost my enchantment with computer hardware. In 1973 I joined Altergo Software, a start-up division of a consulting and contract staffing company. We focused on productivity tools for users of IBM mainframe computers. This early start in engineering gave me the tools and a world view that has stayed with me throughout my career, and provided a lens into the evolution of IT management.

Phase 2—Business Leader
Timing is everything, and 1973 was a good time to be entering the software business! Our company grew quickly. I was fortunate to rise through the ranks and soon I was managing software development, sales, and marketing. I began traveling throughout Europe, opening and supporting distributors for our products.

In 1978 I moved with my family from London, England to Boston, Massachusetts, USA, to help get our nascent US business off the ground. The plan was for me to stay for one year, but 41 years later I am still living in the USA.

Phase 3—Management Consultant
In 1985 our company was acquired by INSAC Group, a British government venture established to promote British computer technology. They were looking to enter the US market through an established British software firm. Altergo Software fit that bill.

I was not thrilled to be working for some far-off bureaucrats, even though they were well-intentioned. I decided to leave, and started a research and consulting business focused on software development automation. I made that decision based on my knowledge of that space and my belief that a lot of help was needed by users of software development automation.

Recognizing the growing interest in computer aided software engineering (CASE), we quickly focused there, and re-named the company CASE Research Corporation. I found myself spending much of my time traveling worldwide, consulting with IT leaders and major management consulting firms. We also published a series of research papers and reports on CASE tools and technologies.

CASE Research grew until, in 1990, it was acquired by Ernst & Young (technically, we merged!). I was admitted as a partner in their newly established Center for Business Innovation and worked alongside world-class luminaries — of the stature of Dr. Tom Davenport and Dr. Philip Pyburn — and with university professors, leading a global research practice focused on IT effectiveness and organizational change.

By 1995 the entrepreneurial itch led me to leave E&Y and the Center for Business Innovation. With two colleagues, I started Omega Point, a company that was to create technology to help companies manage organizational change. Unfortunately, we soon found that obtaining funding was more challenging than we had expected. We drifted into consulting to help pay the bills. This was fine as a stop-gap, but I felt that, if I was going to return to consulting, I needed a more substantial platform. In 1997, I joined a start-up called The Concours Group, led by the remarkable Dr. Ron Christman.

Concours was structured as an integrated business. Although we had research, management consulting, and executive education divisions, most of us worked across these divisions. In a typical week, I would be at our research center in Boston on a Monday and Tuesday — working with a research team on a multi-company research initiative — then on Wednesday and Thursday I would be working with a consulting client. On Friday and through the weekend, I'd be at a resort such as Pebble Beach Golf Club where we held our executive education and networking events. (Dr. Christman was an avid and world-class amateur golfer!)

I found Concours to be a fantastic home for me. I learned through the research, enlightened our member clients through the executive education, and helped clients put ideas into practice through management consulting. Each aspect informed and reinforced the others. We engaged leading academics in our research — people such as Dr. James Cash and Harvard Business School professors, Jim Collins, Gary Hamel, and

Clayton Christenson—and sometimes included them in our consulting engagements.

Entrepreneur and Blogger
Concours was acquired by BSG Alliance in 2007 and went through several rapid name changes, ending as Moxie Software. In 2009 I decided to leave to start my own consulting business—The Merlyn Group.

Embracing Learning and Change
In my career I reinvented myself multiple times: from engineer to manager to business leader to management consultant to researcher to teacher and to author. My multiple reinventions, my work helping IT organizations improve their performance, and my experiences in the performing arts have informed this book.

Through the nature of the consulting work that I've done, I have become highly sensitized and thoughtful about learning and change. I consider them to be two sides of the same coin.

In my teens, in addition to fixing electrical and electronic devices, cars, and motorcycles, I played guitar in a rock and roll band. My father persuaded me to take the university degree path rather than try to be a rock star. At the time, I was not thrilled by this advice, but I knew it made sense.

Many years later (in 2005) I took a short sabbatical from management consulting and went to a Rock 'n' Roll Fantasy Camp in Hollywood, CA, to try to rekindle my musical aspirations. As described earlier, this incredible learning experience led me back to the musical journey I had abandoned 35 years earlier.

Standing on the Shoulders of Giants
One of the most important aspects of my career is that I have worked with many remarkable people. I am an avid researcher and synthesizer of ideas, so rubbing shoulders with talented people has been a career-spanning source of inspiration. I have been blessed with being able to (sometimes, somewhat) connect the dots, see patterns, and help make sense of all the changes going on around me.

If this curated collection of writings is of value to you, it is the minds I have mined that deserve the lion's share of the credit. But I'll gladly take any credit given to me for helping spread the word! The Acknowledgements section of this book has more information about some of those giants and their influence. I am indebted to them for their positive impact on my career.

Acknowledgements

I hardly know where to start this section. I doubt the phrase "standing on the shoulders of giants" has ever been more apt!

I must start with the person without whom this book would not exist. Cheryl White recognized the need and opportunity to adapt my years of blog postings into a book. Beyond planting the seed, Cheryl has been my editor, coach, and guide through the entire processes. Throughout, she demonstrated finely honed consulting and coaching skills. I don't think I've ever seen them more effectively applied.

Thank you to my colleague and business partner, Roy Youngman, who so patiently enlightened me as to the ways of architecture, learning, and human nature. Many of the ideas in this book were jointly developed with Roy through many years of partnership. More accurately, they were often his ideas that I helped to refine.

Recognition goes out to my team at the Ernst & Young Center for Business Innovation: Rick Swanborg, Mary Silva Doctor, Sheila Smith, Nancy Wendt, Charles Gold, and our fearless leader, Bud Mathaisel. Their contributions to the early and important research into IT performance and transformation are embedded in the foundations of the Digital IT Operating Model.

Much of my thinking and learning was shaped by my 12+ years at The Concours Group under the brilliant leadership of the late Dr. Ron Christman. His business model for a firm that would research, educate, and consult to member companies was the perfect incubator for collaboration, innovation and forging so many important relationships with business leaders and leading academics.

Many thanks to my BRM Institute co-founders—Aaron Barnes and Dr. Aleksandr Zhuk—and all the Institute members and staff who helped bring the vision to reality. We goaded and encouraged each other to take the collective plunge and create an organization dedicated to inspiring the world through Business Relationship Management. It seemed like a stretch at the time, but the results have exceeded our loftiest expectations.

My "partners in crime," Kip Fanta, Steve Plante, Peter Lijnse, and Starla Borges deserve a shout out for working with me on the BRM journey. They helped bring my ideas about relationship management to life.

I would also like to recognize all my consulting and training clients over the years. You thought you were learning from me, but it was often the other way around!

Big thanks to my reviewers and their generosity in sharing their time, experience and wisdom in providing invaluable feedback. I wish I had the time and space to include every suggestion!

Last but by no means least, the role of my family was vital to this project. My wife Gillian and daughter Louise have my deepest gratitude. They put up with my near-constant travel and were okay with the fact that they never really understood what I did. I must also pay tribute to the roles played my long-departed parents who led me to believe that I could do anything I put my mind to.

A salute to all of you. Cheers!

Bibliography

Collins, Jim (2001), *Good to Great: Why Some Companies Make the Leap...and Others Don't*, New York, Harper Collins

Connor, Daryl L. (1993), *Managing at the Speed of Change*, Random House, New York

Erickson, Tamara J. (2008), *Retire Retirement: Career Strategies for the Boomer Generation*, Harvard Business Review Press, Boston

Erickson, Tamara J. *http://www.retire-retirement.com*

Froehlich, Andrew (2015), "Shadow IT: 8 Ways To Cope", Information Week

Godin, Seth, https://seths-blog/2011/01/the-pleasant-reassurance-of-new-words/

Juran, Joseph (1964), *Managerial Breakthrough*, McGraw-Hill Inc., New York

Kotter, John (1995), "Why Transformation Efforts Fail" Harvard Business Review

Lencioni, Patrick (2000), *The Four Obsessions of an Extraordinary Executive: A Leadership Fable*, John Wiley & Sons, San Francisco,

Marvin, Carolyn, *When Old Technologies Were New: Thinking About Electric Communication in the Late Nineteenth Century*, 1988, Oxford University Press, New York

Orlikowski, Wanda J and Hofman, J. Debra (1997), "An Improvisational Model of Change Management: The Case of Groupware Technologies", MIT Sloan Management Review Vol. 38, No. 2, pp. 11–21, Cambridge, Massachusetts Institute of Technology

Pirsig, Robert (1974), *Zen and the Art of Motorcycle Maintenance: An Inquiry into Values*, Harper Collins, New York

Scott-Morgan, Peter (1994), *The Unwritten Rules of the Game: Master Them, Shatter Them, and Break Through the Barriers to Organizational Change*, McGraw-Hill, New York

Stacey, Ralph D (1991), *The Chaos Frontier*, Butterworth-Heinmann, Waltham, MA

Taylor, Frederick W. (1947). *Principles of Scientific Management*, Harper, Publishing, New York

Toffler, Alvin (1980), *The Third Wave*, Bantam Books, New York

Treacy, Michael and Wiersema, Fred (1995), *The Discipline of Market Leaders*, Addison-Wesley, New York

Ulrich, Dave (1996), *Human Resource Champions: The Next Agenda for Adding Value and Delivering Results*, Harvard Business School Press, Boston

Wheatley, Margaret (1992), *Leadership and the New Science: Learning about Organization from an Orderly Universe*, Berrett-Koehler Publishers, San Francisco

White, C. L. (2012), *Change On Demand: The Science of Turbo Charging Change in Millennium Corporations*, Eddlesen & Rowe, Denver

Index

CPSIA information can be obtained
at www.ICGtesting.com
Printed in the USA
LVHW061549300820
664592LV00003B/97